BLACK
POWER
INC.

BLACK POWER INC.

The New Voice of Success

Cora Daniels

WILEY

John Wiley & Sons, Inc.

Published by John Wiley & Sons, Inc., Hoboken, New Jersey.
Published simultaneously in Canada.

For general information on our other products and services please contact our Customer Care Department within the United States at (800) 762-2974, outside the United States at (317) 572-3993 or fax (317) 572-4002.

Wiley also publishes its books in a variety of electronic formats. Some content that appears in print may not be available in electronic books. For more information about Wiley products, visit our web site at www.wiley.com.

Library of Congress Cataloging-in-Publication Data:

Daniels, Cora.
  Black Power Inc. : the new voice of success / Cora Daniels.
     p. cm.
  ISBN 0-471-47090-2 (cloth : alk. paper)
  1. African American executives.   2. Career development—United States.
3. Success in business—United States.   4. African Americans—Social
conditions—21st century.   5. United States—Social conditions—21st
century.   I. Title.
HD38.25.U6 D36 2004
658.4′09′08996073—dc22

                                                          2003025143

Printed in the United States of America.

10 9 8 7 6 5 4 3 2 1

For my brother, Omar, the musician,
who continues to teach me the power of a dream.
Blow that horn!

Acknowledgments

Books can be very misleading. My name is on the title page, but many thank-yous are in order to those who helped make this happen; I could not have done it by myself.

Thanks to each and every one of the post-civil rights babies and the executives I have met and talked to through this project. Thank you for sharing your stories, your thoughts, your time, and your lives. Your power and wisdom made my job easy. This book exists because of you.

In that vein, I must also thank Mario Price and Susan Chapman for their never-ending Rolodexes and continued support. The two of you might think of trading in your powerful careers and instead hanging "Source" on your doors because the network of contacts at your fingertips is amazing.

Thanks to John Wiley & Sons for making my first book a reality. Thanks to my editors, Airié Stuart and Linda Witzling: Airié for believing that I had a story worth writing and Linda for working into the night too many times to make this book happen and for being so protective of my voice along the way. Thanks also to Emily Conway and Michelle Patterson for their enthusiasm and dedication. I am forever grateful to the entire team.

Heartfelt thanks to my friend and agent Nicholas Roman Lewis for insisting that I was an author before I realized myself that I was ready. I couldn't have done this without your constant faith and encouragement. You are a great friend and a great agent and I am lucky to have you as both.

Thanks also must go to my mom, Marjorie Horowitz— my biggest cheerleader. It is *me* who loves *you* "totally and completely." Thanks for honestly believing I can do anything. Thanks to my brother, Omar Daniels, for being not just the best "lil' bro," but my friend. I would never give back a single day of our bunk-bed years together on East 6th Street. To my late father, Reginald Daniels, the original master of observation and from whom I inherited any of that skill: I know you are not missing any of this because everyday I can feel your love, Papa. Thank you.

I must also thank one of my oldest friends, John L. Jackson Jr., who constantly pushed me and helped me make it through the pages of my earliest drafts. It is easy to say thank-you for your invaluable insight, eye, and encouragement. It is much harder to find the words to thank you for your friendship; the value of that is immeasurable.

Throughout my career, there have been some notables. The seed for this book was planted when I was heading up a project for *Fortune* magazine called "The 50 Most Powerful Black Executives in America." It was the first time the magazine took on such an awesome endeavor, so thanks for the opportunity. I'd also like to thank Roy S. Johnson for challenging me—my views, ideas, and words. Thanks for constantly making me think. And thanks to Kimberly L. Allers for your generous heart during my book adventures and for making the workday not so much work.

I am grateful to my strong circle of friends, new and old, from Sekou Kaalund for your constant "How's-the-book-comin'?" encouragements to Carol X. Vinzant for never forgetting to check up on me even though I haven't had much time for field trips lately. Thanks to the entire circle.

Thanks most of all to my husband, Rondai Evans, the most powerful Black man I know. I could never do anything that I do without you and your unwavering support. You are my inspiration. Thanks for gladly reading every word I ever

ACKNOWLEDGMENTS

write, including this book several times over, and for listening
to every crazy idea that I have as if it is always something
worth listening to. Thanks for your hard work and putting up
with nights, weekends, and free moments without me over
this past year as *Black Power Inc.* took over our life. And thank
you for your love.

   To all, my deepest gratitude.

Contents

Introduction

*A*nyone who says race doesn't matter is, without a doubt, lying.

Folks who say they don't "see" race. Those who insist they don't notice color. The ones who proudly claim to be color-blind. Lying. Lying. Lying.

Race is something we all notice. No matter what we say, at first glance we are all reduced to race and gender. It is the same as noticing whether someone is bald or brunette. You register whether you are looking at a man or a woman and whether the person's skin is darker or lighter than your own. Admit it.

I was stuck on the subway one day with a cop and the non-stop blaring of his two-way radio. It was like a little window to the chaos that was going on aboveground. "Male Black" barked from the radio continuously as if the phrase were the latest must-say slang dripping from everyone's lips: Male Black this; Male Black that; Male Black here; Male Black there. Generally, subway etiquette dictates keeping your head down and staying quiet. So the "Male Black" barking from the cop's radio was the only voice in the car. It was unavoidable. It occurred to me that the New York Police Department was at least honest about what we all see. Seated next to me was Female White. Across was Male Hispanic. Next to him, Male Hispanic. A few seats over, Female Black. Getting off the train, Female Asian. In the corner, Male Black. Standing up, Male White. Cops say it. The rest of us are just, oh, so polite. But, today our Blackness or whiteness does matter. How much so depends on the person doing the noticing.

I set out to talk to the post-civil rights generation to find out what the biggest beneficiaries of integration are noticing.

This is the first generation to be born and raised after the end of the civil rights movement. As a result, the new generation of Black professionals—those in their mid-30s and younger—are part of a Black elite too many to count. They have the degrees, connections, experiences, and résumés that those before them breaking the color barrier could have only dreamed about.

So I spent months talking to Black 20- and 30-somethings. There was a 33-year-old venture capitalist, a 30-year-old investment banker, and a 28-year-old federal reserve bank examiner, to name a few. I can't forget the 34-year-old CEO, the 25-year-old technology VP, and the 31-year-old Wall Street trader, to name a few more. Then, too, there were the marketing executives, consultants, and corporate attorneys. In the end, I talked to almost 50 well-educated and highly successful young Black executives from across the country doing just about everything.

This group is now gaining its footing in the nation's biggest corporations and law firms, traditional bastions of power, or starting their own companies. I shied away from teachers, artists, government, and nonprofit professionals because their mission or purpose is more readily apparent. Any save-the-world mantra is hard to miss. Instead, I focused on the business world because I wanted to talk to people who are breaking new ground and whose motives aren't as obvious. I was interested in those who are achieving heights that were unthinkable before the civil rights era. I am a journalist by trade, not an anthropologist. So the names I use are real. These are real people at their real companies, being real honest. Not everyone I talked to is identified by name in these pages; but behind every person mentioned, dozens of unnamed others are nodding their heads in agreement.

These Black executives are significant because they have the income and positions that usually reap influence in this country. If money and status equal power, then this group is getting set for a revolution. Whereas previous generations might have gone into government or the church to make a difference, this generation is pouring through freshly opened doors in the corporate world. These are the people who could be the powerbrokers of tomorrow. And no one else is talking to them today.

Pssst . . . here's a secret. After a lifetime of integration, race still matters for the post-civil rights generation. It matters a lot. It matters more. Why is race so important to a generation that has had more opportunity than any before? The first generation born after Martin Luther King Jr.'s dream of little Black boys and Black girls joining hands with little white boys and white girls is more likely to embrace a world that the civil rights generation fought so hard to destroy. Back then, segregation was always bad and integration was always good. The fight was for the right to make choices, but the unspoken assumption was that in the end everyone would make the same choice. But, for post-civil rights babies, things are not so, well, black and white. The segregation bad/integration good equation does not necessarily ring true. Instead, this generation embraces a Black world of shared culture, shared experience, and shared history—by choice.

This is what I learned talking to the current crop of Black professionals—the most successful, well-educated, biggest beneficiaries of integration, the group that some argue has overcome race.

Truth is, they've already watched a generation of Black executives do whatever they had to do to get ahead. The previous generation molded themselves into good corporate soldiers—long hours, good work, and most important, no waves. The groundbreaking generation of Black executives tried their hardest not to make an issue of race in the office because, for the most part, they were just thankful to be let in. Their mission was to prove that they could be like everyone else.

But then they didn't get very far. This is not to say that they didn't climb high. There are some very powerful Black executives in corporate America. They include Stan O'Neal, CEO of Merrill Lynch, the nation's largest brokerage firm; Franklin Raines, CEO of Fannie Mae, the mortgage finance company that is at the heart of the U.S. economy; and Ann Fudge, CEO of Young & Rubicam, the first Black woman to head a major advertising firm. But, most did not manage to break through all the glass ceilings at the very top. Instead, the plateau for many was somewhere in senior management, which is overloaded with responsibility but has little influence. Many more became frustrated, or worse, were consumed by their frustration.

As a result, the post-civil rights generation is not convinced that the sacrifices demanded by the so-called color-blind corporate world are worth it. Partly this is because they want to go farther faster. Assimilation and diminishing the role of race are not options for this generation. Frankly, young Black executives don't want their Blackness to be ignored, especially in the office. They have concluded that race cannot and should not be eliminated. In fact, this generation is driven by race.

Success in a white world has become the means to an end. And that end is different from the one sought by the groundbreakers like Stan O'Neal. They are not trying to climb the ladder to see how far they can go in the white world but are merely interested in *power*. The mantra with each move is not "Will this help me here, at this company?" but "Will this help me help Black folks out there?" This generation's goal is to build the wealth of a people, because with that comes power.

Therefore they are not marching or protesting or thinking of uplifting the community one block at a time. Their aim is not to integrate or make corporate America—the white business world—more diverse. Instead, they are using their access to once-forbidden worlds for themselves—to learn what they can and enjoy the benefits of their knowledge.

These executives are building funds and controlling assets, using the dollar to improve education and wield influence, political and otherwise. They are also gaining independence for the community by starting their own companies. When this generation volunteers its time and services on the block, they are trying to spread the knowledge they gained from walking through those doors. This is what Black Power Inc., the movement, is about.

In talking about this generation, I noticed that lots of people want to be part of "post-civil rights." A friend who is squarely in the 40-something bracket took offense when I deemed him too old to be part of the post-civil rights generation, as I define it. But I *am*, he protested! Yet, he could vividly recall when his dad took the family to the local diner and sat down at the counter for a meal for the first time after the "White Only" sign was lifted. The 20- and 30-somethings have none of those memories. And that's the difference.

Sure, those in their 40s and 50s came of age for the most part after the darkest "For Colored Only" days of the era. But they could still touch a time when the upheaval existed and blood was being shed in the streets over race. Even if they were just seeing images on the news, the struggle was real because it was happening in the present tense. No matter how hard this current generation may try, they can't have that connection. Anything they have heard or seen did not occur in their lifetime. It is history. That is what being *post* means.

A child who was 6 years old in 2001 will live most of his life post-9/11. But he is not post. That tragedy took place in his young lifetime. He will have memories of *something*, even if it is just a mood swing in his home far, far away from New

York City, Washington, D.C., or a field in Pennsylvania. It might be just a flash of his parents watching TV about something **big** going on. It doesn't matter; that flash makes him different from a baby born in 2002. That baby has no experience of how different life once was, no matter how many times she learns about it in school. Everything that baby has done, including being born, has been afterward. Like the 2002 baby, the post-civil rights generation holds no memories of life before and exists in the new world that has come afterward.

My friend wasn't the only 40-something to do the "Me Too" dance. It was actually more common than not. The generation of groundbreakers—the first wave of Black executives to reach prominence in corporate America—from senior vice presidents in their 40s up through Dick Parsons, CEO of Time Warner, all tried to tell me that they are post-civil rights, too. This group definitely sees a difference between their generation and the next generation but thinks it has claim to the label because of when they came of age. I see their argument, but I still think they are like that 6-year-old in 2001.

It is interesting how common the "Me Too" dance is. Some of it might be mid-life crisis angst. But, I think, most of it is a natural attempt to be part of that which looks forward and not backward. Civil rights, even in all its glory, is our history. Inherently, anything post is the future.

Even though Tom Jones is one of the most senior Black executives on Wall Street, his name and his history don't usually ring many bells. As the CEO in charge of global investments, private banking, and asset management for Citigroup, the Me Too executive oversees 12,000 employees and almost $700 billion in assets. But Jones rose to national prominence in 1969 as the leader of an armed student revolt at Cornell University.

Cornell in 1969 proved to be the setting of one of the most notorious campus revolts during the era of campus revolts. Black students, alienated and full of anger, decided to organize around the campus's racial chasm. The list of demands was long, ranging from asking for a Black Studies department to calling for the university to divest itself of investments in South Africa as its peers had done. During Parents Weekend, the day after a cross was burned outside a Black dorm, 100 Black students armed with guns stormed the student union. Tom Jones, a quiet respectful, nonthreatening 19-year-old senior from Brooklyn studying regional planning, led the way. The resulting standoff lasted 35 hours. After spending the night on the floor clutching a rifle, Jones emerged before a nervous crowd of nearly 6,000 members of the Cornell community. It was exactly 3 minutes after 8 P.M. when he addressed the mostly white audience: "In the past it has been the Black people who have done the dying," he said. "Now has come the time when the pigs are going to die too. We are moving tonight. Cornell has until 9 P.M. to live."

Cornell President James Perkins ended up out of a job. Jones landed on the cover of *Newsweek* as the symbol of a movement.

After graduation, Jones traded in his rifle for a business career. He started knocking down corporate doors in 1971 when most of the post-civil rights babies were, well, really babies. His earliest corporate job was with Ernst & Young, as one of its first Black accountants.

"I came to corporate America," he says, "after proving to the world that I could potentially lead an armed revolution."

The key word here is *after*.

Jones sees the revolt as very much a part of the past. The post-civil rights generation sees the revolution as ongoing. There is no "after" . . . yet. The fight is not over. These days Jones shies away from issues of race, by any means necessary. "We essentially live in a colorblind society now, especially for the elites of America," he told me one day. Even more so than his rifle-toting past, it is that color-blind attitude that really makes Jones a generation away from post-civil rights. Tom Jones *is* history, then. Now, it is time to meet the future.

So what is *Black Power Inc.,* the book, about? It is the story of the post-civil rights generation and race. The success of this generation is fueled by their refusal to check their Blackness at the door. In Chapter 1, "Working While Black," enter the world of these young Black executives. Race is the coworker that we usually try to ignore at the office. For this generation, that is not so easy.

In Chapter 2, "Beyond Rage," learn how this generation is turning frustration into a movement. They are not trying to knock down doors anymore but to take advantage of the doors already open.

Chapter 3, "Sistas Unite!" points out that Black women are the ones who are filling the executive ranks of tomorrow at greater rates. Black women, who are often more emboldened about race then their male counterparts, are poised to be the leaders of tomorrow.

Chapter 4, "Dissed by Diversity," explores the hoax of corporate diversity programs. American corporations have accepted these programs because they dismiss race by extending the definition of diversity to embrace everyone.

Chapter 5, "Generational Warfare," reveals the friction between the generations of Black professionals. Dick Parsons, Time Warner CEO, and Ken Chenault, American Express CEO, talk about the next wave of Black executives trying to fill their shoes.

Chapter 6, "This Generation Needs No Leaders," challenges conventional concepts of success and leadership. Instead of putting out an APB for the next Black leader, young Black executives are using the benefits gained by the civil rights movement to become leaders themselves.

Chapter 7, "What Does All This mean for Main Street?" talks about how race shapes this generation's goals. Black business has become the foundation for the next Black Power movement. These highly educated, corporate-trained, Black entrepreneurs have one thing in mind: toppling Main Street to build Black wealth.

Chapter 8, "Separate but Equal," deals with life after work—where we live, socialize, network—and the movement to stay separate.

The post-civil rights generation is also my generation. I am a post-civil rights baby. Coming of age in the late 1970s and 1980s, I could sit at the front of the bus, eat at the lunch counter, and sip from any water fountain I found. In my lifetime, "Nigger" became the N-word and "Nigga" a Black teenage term of endearment. At 18, I could register to vote without anyone noticing and could even expect to see Black faces on the ballot. Being post-Affirmative Action, I went to integrated schools and was able to earn two Ivy League degrees. I live in an age when even the census bureau no longer requires us to check just one box for race. I am post race riots, post assassinations, and post we-shall-overcome marches.

Lastly, I set out to talk to my generation because it is on the cusp of power. It is about to make its move. I wanted to give the post-civil rights babies a chance to finally speak. To speak unclouded by assumptions and without the weight of expectations.

So listen. . . .

PROLOGUE:
WHAT ARE YOU?

*W*hat are you?

The question was shot at me from across the table one day in the cafeteria. I remember his unremarkable brown hair and his bowl haircut. It was 1979, and we were in the third grade. I remember his brown-and-orange striped turtleneck, too, because I was still at the stage where a turtleneck was punishment. By lunchtime if I had been wearing that mother-approved wintertime neck jail, the choking feeling would've already gotten too unbearable to speak. The question cut through the squeals, laughter, whispers, and open-mouth chewing going on in the cafeteria, stinging my ears as it landed. The trail of silence was so uncomfortable that even a swig of apple juice and a fistful of Pepperidge Farm Goldfish couldn't have helped. What are you? I could think of lots of answers. What are you? A nerd who every day matched the different colored ballies in her hair to her socks. What are you? The hopscotch champion of East 6th street and probably beyond. What are you? A girl who could ride a 10-speed just as fast as her brother. What are you? A truthfully shy kid who did not want to be bothered.

But, there was no mistaking what he meant.

It definitely wasn't the first time I had heard those three words. But it was probably the first time that I realized the importance of the question. People have been asking it my entire life. They ask confused. They ask accusingly. Noses twist up and eyes squint as if it is my fault that they don't know the answer at first glance. Not that it is a mystery, except to those doing the asking. The truth is "What are you?" is really a polite way of asking if you are one of *us* or one of *them*. That's how race is. It divides and unites. And, even in the third grade, it always matters.

What are you?

Third grade was the year of Mrs. Howard at P.S. 41 in the heart of Greenwich Village, New York City. That year, my class learned everything through the eyes of Africa. Mrs. Howard had been on safari the summer before and was still obsessed with faraway homelands. The highlight of the year was when we made "African" huts from clay. My dad never did get rid of mine even though the grass roof turned brown and started balding almost immediately. At the time, the Village was the liberal epicenter. It was the bohemian focal point where artists, lifestyles, and political angst intermingled freely. Individuality and creativity were hailed as birthrights. In terms of all getting along, it wasn't a matter of "Can we," but "We can." Technically, my family lived too far East–too close to the projects of Alphabet City and the tenements of the Lower East Side–to be legitimate residents of the Village bubble. But for school, my brother and I abandoned our gritty blocks and snuck across district lines every morning to be a part of that educational melting pot.

At my Village school, we had Black kids, white kids, kids who celebrated Christmas, Hanukkah, both, and absolutely nothing, not to mention Kwanzaa, and Ramadan. There were kids who spoke Spanish at home and kids who spoke Chinese at school. Kids who wore veils every day at a time when none of us knew what terrorists were. Kids who only saw Daddy every other weekend and could drop phrases in the school-yard like "child support" just as easily as "you're it." Kids who were being raised by two mommies and those who were secretly jealous because they didn't have even one. Just kids.

What are you?

That day in the cafeteria there were no Chinese-speaking, Kwanzaa-celebrating kids with two mommies at the table—just me and a sea of bowl haircuts. I had a table full of ears at my control, and for the quietest girl in the class, that was scarier than everything else in the cafeteria. What are you? The question was asked because my answer mattered. That is why the sea was listening. Even in the third grade, smack in the middle of the melting pot of Greenwich Village in New York City, my race was important.

Guessing always followed "What are you?" After making a few stops across the globe (the usual safety of Puerto Rico was immediately rejected since I could speak less Spanish than the kids with nannies), the crowd was getting restless. The moment was dragging. Then, just when attention spans were running out, "Ooh! Ooh! Ooh! I know! I know!" Someone was bursting with an answer.

"She's mixed" . . .

Even at the time, that phrase didn't make that much sense to me. *Mixed* is a generation removed from *mulatto* and a step before *biracial* and then *multicultural*. All I knew was that I had never heard of any People's Republic of Mixed before. There was no "Mixed" hut I could make for my Dad. Besides, weren't all kids a mixture of their mother and father? Sure my Mom was white and Jewish and from a tiny town in Virginia, and my Dad was Black and Methodist and from the big city of Chicago. But, that didn't mean I was mixed (up). So, I corrected the crowd in the know-it-all tone of an 8-year-old and told every-one: "I am Black." It wasn't any big realization, political state-ment, or power-to-the-people affirmation. My parents never sat me down and discussed it with me. Race wasn't ignored in my house, but it wasn't taught either. Race was just a part of living—for any kid. And even in third-grade logic, it seemed simply ob-vious. If the kid with the bowl haircut and twisted-up nose was asking me the question, then I couldn't possibly be the same as him (and didn't want to be).

This wasn't a discovery of my Blackness. I always knew and was comfortable with who I am. While growing up, I never wanted straight hair, never wanted blue eyes; and even in the sixth grade during a lesson on body image, I was the only girl in the class who thought her butt was her best body part. In my racial memory, there are also much more painful events, including the usual benchmarks of nigger calling and overt discrimination. But that moment at the cafeteria table, I realized that my Blackness mattered to *everyone else*. That is es-pecially true for the generation of post-civil rights babies.

Born in the 1970s and coming of age in the 1980s, we were the first generation completely molded after the fight for racial equality was supposed to be over. There were no more marches and no counters where we couldn't sit. On the evening news, we saw no images of the defiant being hosed down. We were the kids who were supposed to enjoy the integrated paradise that all that marching was for. New York City is perhaps the most diverse city in the world, and the Village was the heart of that. But it is naive to think that race doesn't matter, even in this bubble. That someone could ask me the question that day in the cafeteria is a sign that it matters even more, for both sides. The kids doing the asking were not bowing to tradition and so-cial norms. Their curiosity was natural—what are you? They honestly wanted to know, because it matters. We all wanted to know. Usually race is apparent immediately without asking, so it is easy to overlook that we still take note. And I answered the question because race isn't a secret to be hidden, but something to be proud of and celebrated. Even third graders had already learned that lesson.

The difference between the racial consciousness of the post-civil rights generation and those that came before was that we were supposed to have been beyond the Black power stage. We were supposed to enjoy and take advantage of this brave new world presented to us. We could finally be invited to the party, and damn it, we were supposed to enjoy it. The only thing is, my generation still had to fight. Instead of wearing white sheets and burning crosses, our attackers were camouflaged. The full-pronged assault could come from anywhere and everywhere. That is why boys with bowl haircuts and brown-and-orange turtlenecks could eat lunch with you *and* ask, What are you? My generation argues that the sting of a sneak attack lasts longer. The only thing you can do to survive is to hold on to yourself. Pride is a survival tactic. Thus, race becomes not just who you are but your reason for being. When we were finished fighting, we didn't much care about being invited anymore. We wanted to throw the parties instead.

The year after I answered the question in the cafeteria, Ronald Reagan was elected president and would rule for the formative years of my generation's racial awakening. Reagan's rocky relationship with the Black community has already been well documented, so there is no need to rehash old news here. But, a few highlights might illustrate the racial climate that we post-civil rights babies were blossoming in.

Shortly after the Republican Convention, Reagan kicked off his campaign with a speech in Philadelphia, Mississippi. This small patch of Mississippi was where Klansmen had murdered three civil rights workers 16 years before in one of the most notorious episodes of the 1960s. In 1980, Reagan stood in Philadelphia, Mississippi, and delivered a speech proclaiming his support of "states' rights." For any student of history, the phrase, which was popularized by the segregation Dixiecrat campaign of 1948, is racist code for anti-Black. The reference is so fraught with historic innuendo that a white southern audience could not possibly miss it. That's how the candidate *started*. As president, Reagan cut budgets for the Equal Opportunities Commission (EOC) by 24 percent in his first term. The Justice Department filed only one school desegregation case. The president also opposed both the Civil Rights Act and the Voting Rights Act. Before leaving office, Reagan had also coined his own racist code: "welfare queen."

By the time the post-civil rights generation was in high school at the end of the decade, I had been through a truckload of "what are yous." Now the stakes were higher, though; futures were at risk. Affirmative action was fully under fire. Quotas became code for unqualified. Everyone felt as if they were owed something, but were not getting anything. During my senior year, honors kids, divided along racial lines, were getting into brawls à la *West Side Story* over college rejections and SAT scores. There was no more melting pot bubble. People chose sides, said the unsaid, and friendships were broken forever. A message scrawled in my yearbook offered "congrats" and assurance that I deserved my Ivy League acceptance "even though" I was Black.

The hidden attack was definitely winning. We got to college angry, bitter, defensive, and gladly seeking the comfort of our own. For four years, I barely socialized with anyone who wasn't a card-carrying member of the African American Cultural Center. My cocooning was typical, not the exception. "The House," as we called it, hosted parties and lectures, organized and disorganized, of all things Black. It was one of several ethnic oases on campus. A safe *Cheers*-like place away from home, where we belonged. It was no different from the Hillel house, drama clique, or soccer boys except that we clung to race. However, before going away to school, most of us had come from integrated environments.

In college, instead of "What are you?" being hurled across the lunch table, I heard Nigger hurled from a passing car late at night on my way home from the library. Fellow students would casually ask Black classmates for IDs before letting them enter their dorm. On the news, there were stories about fraternities holding mock slave auctions during rush week. Each year on Halloween, there was always someone sporting an Afro and Blackface—as if pairing that with a basketball jersey would make it okay.

Because none of this was supposed to still be happening, my generation unified around race. Emblazoned on the front of a popular T-shirt at the time was Malcolm X clutching a rifle; on the back was printed: "It's a Black Thang, You wouldn't understand." I would wear my shirt to football games for maximum display. Picking apart that phrase is interesting, though. My generation had moved beyond *Black Is Beautiful,* a statement of pure affirmation and pride. Instead, "It's a Black Thang" directly challenges others with its pride by clearly signaling that not everyone is welcomed or invited.

The difference between this militancy of the post-civil rights generation and the actions of those who came before is that, after graduation, we took our Ivy League degrees and went to work on Wall Street, at the Fortune 500, and at topflight law firms. One of the most "down brothas" at college, who could inspire a crowd with angry defiance of the Man over *anything,* took his engineering degree to Procter & Gamble. Last I heard he could still stir a crowd, but he was now a respectable high-level vice president.

We just put suits on over our T-shirts.

9

These days, school cafeterias are a distant memory. But people have never stopped asking me that question: coworkers and strangers and both. The continuing question is a constant reminder how much it all still matters. Long past the third grade, the office is now the battlefield. The repercussions are greater because money is involved. But now the swell of young Black executives is significant enough to have my back.

So, what am I? I'm a Black woman. Now what?

1

WORKING WHILE BLACK

There is definitely a look of surprise by someone I've never met when I walk into the room to run a meeting. Or in the parking lot you'll notice some people are nervous or tense up as I pass. It's not my suit or briefcase they are reacting to so it must be the color of my skin.

> —Oral Muir, a 33-year-old e-commerce executive with
> Marriott Hotel, on being a Black man in the office.

*B*linking in my inbox one day, there it was—a Fwd and Fwd and Fwd e-mail that had already been around a few times. Fwd e-mails are pure indulgence—messages that your friends want you to read, but that contain nothing you really have to read. They are irresistible that way. The subject line of this latest e-mail making its way through corporate America read—rather screamed—*Working While Black!* Despite my best effort, I couldn't help but smile. Not a Kool-Aid grin moment. But more a nod your head, I feel-your-pain, collective lip curve. All those Fwds signaled that I wasn't alone.

The e-mail was a Letterman-like list of 20 workplace scenarios that included the following:

Working While Black

3. A colleague says with a broad smile, "You know I really like you. When I see you, I don't see color. I don't think of you as Black."
9. You arrive at an off-site business retreat dressed in business casual attire. Your non-person-of-color peers approach and ask, "Why are you always so dressed up?"

11. You are frequently asked why you change your hair-style so often.
14. After a coworker returns from a weekend in the sun, they run to you on Monday morning and extend their arms to touch yours and say, "Hey, I'm darker than you."

There goes that collective lip curve again.

Isolated, overlooked, ignored—that is what Working While Black (WWB) means. And it's not funny. For young Black professionals, it is a cage. Some successful Black 30-somethings joke about the "5-year meltdown." It takes about 5 years after business school for their fellow Black executives to feel as if they are suffocating in the cage. Optimism dissolves and hope shatters. It usually starts with the pace at which they are moving up the ladder—it is not as fast as they think it should be. It then turns into more. Earning respect in the office, as a Black executive, is more of a battle than they expected. Also the daily struggle of trying to fit into corporate environments that reward conformity can be trying for any group that is different. The internal torment can wreak havoc on the mind and emotions. These young Black executives still succeed in the office, but their spirit has been damaged. Trapped in the cage, they become angry and fed up. The culmination of the meltdown occurs when they start asking themselves the dangerous question: What am I doing?

Working While Black is not a rant, not a boo-hoo fest, not a plea for help, and not a sign of giving up. In the twenty-first century, it is just the truth.

"Black people have been holding onto this fairy tale bill of goods for too long," says Sean Hudson, a 34-year-old marketing exec at Bristol-Myers Squibb (BMS). "Be realistic. We are Black people in corporate America. Sure, we are making way more than our folks ever made. But I don't want to wake up and be

45, overqualified and underemployed, and have to think about how I got pimped."

Sean is one of seven. That is what he discovered after a three-day companywide meeting of the pharmaceutical giant's marketing division. They represented every BMS office across the country—from entry level up to senior management. It was the type of exhausting event that straddles the line between useful and not. At one point during the meeting, all 400 or so marketing professionals gathered together in the auditorium. Only seven were Black. So Sean is one of seven. He works in the HIV division trying to get physicians and health care professionals to sign onto the latest HIV drugs developed by BMS.

Sean spouted his precious *pimped* line one day when he called me from the Pittsburgh airport. During a conversation that seemed more therapy session than research, he unloaded about being the only Black man in too many rooms during his career. His words made my reporter ears immediately perk up in a way that only happens when a great quote is uttered. The feeling of being used at many levels runs rampant among these Black executives, and Sean had expressed it perfectly. Even before we ever met in person, I started dropping the line into conversations with friends. Before I knew it, my whole circle was talking about how we, too, didn't want to get pimped.

When I finally met Sean, he was 32 days away from a big product launch that he was running and 34 estimated days away from fatherhood. The stress radiated from him like blinding sunlight. But he wanted to talk. I wasn't surprised. I get that a lot from this generation of Black executives; they want to talk about race and their place. Cell phones, e-mails, two-way messages—I'd heard from people in the wee hours of the morning, from the middle of office meetings, and from vacation spots. They want to talk because they believe they are the only ones dealing with the frustrations of WWB (they're not). They fear their generation is disjointed and lacking unity (it isn't). And mostly they want to talk because they feel no one is listening (well, maybe). So after the last session of that three-day marketing meeting, well past 8 P.M., Sean stopped by my office to talk before his commute home to his pregnant wife in the suburbs.

The conflict between the 32- and 34-day milestones meant that Sean was going to have to choose whether to witness the birth of his first child or run the product launch meeting that he had been told was critical for his promotion. The "7 of 400 issue," as he refers to it, was gnawing at him: "It scares me." Adding to his resentment was that it was a promotion he felt he had earned and for which he had already been passed over previously. That is why the fear of being pimped is very real. It wasn't the first time the equality fairy tale had been shattered for him during his career. After watching the "hoops of fire" a senior Black executive was put through for a promotion, he concluded: "There are different metrics for different people." Period.

So we talked. Sean tried to convince me that he was not bitter, yet. I tried to believe him. But there was a lot of talk about credentials and limits—the better credentials that this generation of Black professionals brings to the table and the limits the world still puts on them despite those credentials. Adding to Sean's distress over the 7-of-400 issue is that none of those 7 was at a higher level than he is. No Black faces ever graced the stage during the three days. There was no one, he felt, in a position of significant power, authority, or influence. His own department, HIV, is profitable, but it still is just a "pimple on the ass" of BMS. "There is no meritocracy," says Sean emotionless and accepting. "But I am not naive enough to think that there is a place in corporate America that is. The grass isn't significantly greener anywhere else."

Welcome to Working While Black.

Today's reality, in the words of federal researchers, is one in which the "playing field is *still* far from level [italics added]." A recent government study of employment data concluded, "African Americans continue to suffer the most severe extent of intentional job discrimination." The study, which examined 200,000 of the nation's largest and midsize companies, found that overall African Americans have a 41 percent chance of being discriminated against at work no matter what their level or industry. Black professionals and managers in corporate America stand a nearly 30 percent chance of being discriminated against on the job. The research also found that in 1999, the most recent year data was analyzed, 27 percent of the nation's companies visibly discriminated against African Americans. Of those companies, 10 percent, or 22,000, exhibited what the Equal Employment Opportunity Commission (EEOC) terms "Hard Core" discrimination against African Americans, meaning not only that these companies practiced the highest level of employment discrimination recognized by the federal government but that they had also exhibited such discrimination for more than a decade.[1]

Perhaps the most intriguing thing about WWB is that race relations have reached the point that the phrase "While Black" doesn't really need explanation. So here's the Cliff's Notes version: Headlines in the mid-1990s about state police targeting Black motorists along the nation's highways helped pluck the catchall phrase from Black chitchat and inject it into national mainstream vernacular. Driving While Black, Walking While Black, Flying While Black, Learning While Black, [*insert your own verb here*] While Black.

In 1999, during an investigation by the Department of Justice, the state of New Jersey admitted that its state troopers systematically pulled motorists over because of their race. In the eyes of the state, complaints from Black motorists that they were being targeted by police on the New Jersey turnpike were "real, not imagined." An embarrassing photo of Christie Todd Whitman, governor of New Jersey, frisking a young Black hands-against-the-wall man in a mock traffic stop became the new symbol of the Garden State. The State Police Commissioner was eventually forced to step down when he tried to defend the practice of what became known as racial profiling or Driving While Black.

After the publicity in New Jersey, lawsuits in Pennsylvania and along the I-95 corridor including Maryland, Delaware, Florida, and Connecticut legitimized the issue for the nation. This wasn't a case of Black professionals whining about cabs whizzing past them in midtown Manhattan. This was documented discrimination by law enforcement.

"While Black" was everywhere—even in the workplace.

But, few know that Driving While Black actually has traceable roots. Profiling as a police method grew out of the War on Drugs as it began to take shape in the early 1980s. At the time, legislators were faced with out-of-control drug violence. Frustrated by law enforcement's inability to lock up the drug lords behind the underground economy, they shifted their focus onto the kingpins' underlings. Drug couriers and small-time dealers became public enemy number one. Why go after the big fish when the guppies are what really matter, right? In 1985, the Drug Enforcement Administration (DEA) introduced Operation Pipeline, an intelligence program that emphasized the transportation of drugs along the nation's highways, and tried to educate local law enforcement about how to pick out drug couriers. The instructions included general profiles of what these couriers could look like including type of car, patterns of driving, age, and, yes, race. What happened, though, as the lawsuits in the late 1990s illustrate, is that race became the only part of the profile that mattered. Black men became the profile.[2]

Laws were passed to give weight to this new emphasis on the transportation of drugs. Most notable was the Comprehensive Crime Act of 1984, which gave police the right to seize property of suspected drug dealers.[3] The idea was to hit drug dealers where it hurt them most: Take their belongings and ask questions later. The logic behind the seizures was that such property was bought through illegal means—dirty money or underground channels—so it didn't really belong to these drug pushers in the first place. The plan made sense, except the part that threw out the basis of our justice system—the presumption of innocence. So what the beefed-up power of seizure laws really did was give a monetary incentive to local law enforcement to pull people over at the same time that the Feds were providing a profile of *who* to pull over. Interesting.

In 1997, the year before the New Jersey situation prompted politicians from both sides of the aisle to denounce racial profiling, local police and sheriff departments snatched up $648 million in cash, goods, and property from supposed drug traffickers.[4] Impressive, if it weren't for one detail. Eighty percent of those who had assets seized were never charged with any crime.[5] Under federal law, people can be sentenced to a maximum of 5 years in prison for refusing to let cops seize their property during a traffic stop. In essence, police departments quickly learned that they could make money by pulling Black folks over.

If racial profiling is steeped in historical lore, then "While Black" reflects the emotional buildup of all that history. This phrase conveys the shared experience and expectations of Black people created by the active practice of prejudices and stereotypes about race. Simply, it is the baggage that comes with being Black in a white world, period. It is the reason behind the inexplicable. Why is the store manager following me around as I shop? Why am I being seated next to the kitchen at the 5-star restaurant? Why do women clutch their bags when I pass? Why do I feel constantly disrespected in the office? Remembering that I am [Shopping, Sitting, Walking, Working] While Black, is an attempt to provide logic to racist behavior. This all matters in the post-civil rights world because, despite the progress made, at last, the races continue to exist separately and differently making true equality still a dream.

Take housing. The most common measure of residential segregation is the U.S. Census Bureau's dissimilarity index. The index ranges from 0 to 100, where 0 means that African Americans and whites live together in perfectly balanced neighborhoods and 100 indicates complete segregation. Scores greater than 60 are considered to be "high"; those above 70 are "extreme." In 2000, the most recent data available, the average level of Black-White segregation in U.S. cities stood at 64, higher than segregation between any other groups. In the Northeast and the Midwest, the average segregation indices tend to be extreme, standing around 74. Checking in with an index of 85, the most segregated city in the nation is Detroit, birthplace of the automobile and Motown, and apparently still Jim Crow's hometown. Following Detroit's segregated lead are Milwaukee (82); New York (81); Newark, New Jersey (80); and Chicago (also 80). Other areas with extreme segregation scores include Buffalo, New York, Cincinnati, Cleveland, Kansas City, Philadelphia, and St. Louis.

Which means racial segregation is not unique to your county, township, subdivision, or block; or to South Central, Harlem, the South Side, or the Hill District; or to Utah, North Dakota, or Washington State. It is the American way of life. Most other multiracial societies are not as segregated—not Brazil, Canada, or the United Kingdom. The only other place where Black-White segregation indices routinely exceeded 70 was South Africa—under apartheid. Perhaps that bears repeating. Only under the legal segregation of apartheid–a system deemed so backward and heinous in this country that by the late 1980s it inspired widespread protests, mock shantytowns across college campuses, and ultimately congressional sanctions–were things worse.

Given the residential segregation, separate and often not-so-equal schools should not surprise anyone. The heavy hand of the law brought a period of integration to the nation's school districts. After schools began desegregating in the mid-1950s, they became steadily more integrated until the late 1980s. But then as more conservative courts began to strike down bussing and forced integration programs, the trend started to slow down. Now it is in reverse. Really. The proportion of African Americans attending integrated or majority-white schools declined by 13 percent during the 1990s.[6] That is the lowest level of school integration since 1968. Take a peek at our schoolyards, the lunch tables in the cafeteria, the classrooms. There is no mixing. There is nothing to mix; there are white schools and Black schools. Once you take the time to notice, the extensive sea of sameness can be striking. About the only things more monochromatic are the color choices of the motor vehicle bureau, or maybe the walls of a psychiatric institution. That is a powerful lesson we are teaching our children in almost every school in the nation.

Even in the most integrated city in the United States–Sacramento (according to research conducted by the Civil Rights Project for *Time* magazine)–life is not a multicolored paradise. In this California city, everyone is a minority. Of the city's 407,000 residents, 41 percent are non-Hispanic white, 15.5 percent are Black, 22 percent are Hispanic, and 17.5 percent are Asian. One in every 5 babies born in Sacramento is of mixed racial heritage. Although other cities, such as New York and Los Angeles, are more diverse, Sacramento's innovative housing programs, affordable real estate, and stable supply of traditionally integrated government and college campus employment have encouraged people of different races to actually live side by side. But, even in an integrated wonderland like Sacramento, racial tensions persist. At the local high school, Black and Hispanic parents find themselves pitted against whites and Asians for resources and attention. The police department, although serving a community that includes people who speak more than 70 different languages, is still 70 percent white; in 2000, 27 percent of the drivers stopped were Black, a higher rate than any other group. Says the local NAACP (National Association for the Advancement of Colored People) chapter president, Anne Gayles-White: "There is still too much racism and hatred in a city like this."[7] You get the picture.

But work is what we all have in common as a society. It is the bridge that holds us together. This means that, for too many of us, the workplace often is the only setting where we mingle with different races on a regular basis. We live in our separate communities, send our kids to separate schools, go to separate parties, worship under separate roofs, and even watch separate TV shows. It is the office that disrupts those separate worlds.

Of course, it is still forced interaction. (With discrimination payouts as high as $192 million, segregation is an expensive habit for the Fortune 500.)[8] Still, such interactions, no matter how limited, are where issues of race often get shaped, discussed, and examined. As much as we might try to keep the personal out of the office, it is impossible. Watercooler talk is real. Eventually, opinions slip from even the most reserved tongues. Likes and dislikes are exposed. Questions pop up. Such actions are what make us human. In our lives outside the office, we can control our audience. We surround ourselves with people who, at least, think like us. So, we pretty much know what to expect when such slips seep out. It is like a stacked deck; there is no gamble. But, when we expose our beliefs on the job, the reaction can be unpredictable. It is these unexpected moments—the newness in our world—that have the greatest potential in forming our viewpoints. Observations, real or imagined, become proof. Proof feeds ideas. Ideas lead to behavior.

That makes work an influential place.

The danger is that our views on race are much more emotional than logical. There will never be a scientific equation that can prove our racial conclusions. Instead, these things are based on feel, look, interpretation. There is nothing wrong with that, but the office is not the ideal setting for emotions, and so things constantly churn and bubble. Race is always present. Add money to emotions and people tend to become more sensitive to the race factor of any given moment. That is what work does. Something as little as the competition for a promotion can cause people's prejudices to seep out on one side and militancy to form on the other.

The boys with the bowl haircuts are balding now and ties have replaced the brown-and-orange striped turtlenecks, but the lessons learned in the third grade remain. Race mattered then, race matters now, race matters tomorrow. Saying that it doesn't is like claiming to be unaware whether someone is a man or a woman, tall or short, fat or thin. We could blame things on a person's shortness or thinness, but we just don't. It is against this reality—separate schools, neighborhoods, churches, everything—that While Black develops and flourishes. Only when these separate worlds intersect is While Black possible. Without a white world, While Black could not exist.

Working While Black

1. A coworker sees you and several Black colleagues at a casual lunch. Back at the office she asks, "What was that meeting all about?"

15. Walking through the hall with colleagues, you exchange greetings with two other African Americans you pass along the way. Your colleague says, "My, you know so many people."

Before we continue, a couple of explanations are in order. The first big misconception of integration is that one or two integrates. As long as a group is not 100 percent white, then it is considered integrated. But for those doing the integrating, there is no difference in the everyday world between 100 percent and 95 percent, 90 percent, or even 85 percent. They are still one of a few in a very big pack. That kind of math alone makes them, in essence, always the other.

The other big falsehood of integration is that it works two ways. If a group is 95 percent white, it is considered integrated; but if that same group is 95 percent Black, it is referred to as all Black. Take the sitcoms on UPN. They are often portrayed in the media, and in our minds, as a ghetto marathon of urban comedy. But most have a token white character. On *The Steve Harvey Show,* there's Bullet Head; on *Girlfriends,* there's Toni's fiancé; and *The Parkers* has best friend Stevie. Still, these shows are never considered integrated. Yet, when *Friends* hired Black actress Aisha Tyler just in time for sweeps for a recurring role, media stories the next day were about the integration of NBC's number one sitcom. "Diversity on *Friends,*" splashed one AP story. For a real-world example, consider communities that get hit with white flight. A few years ago, the *Detroit Free Press* examined the issue with a series of high-profile stories. The tone was predictably dire. One article "From white to black: Once an integration model Southfield sees population shift" detailed how 21,000 whites have left the suburb since 1990 as African Americans have moved in. The conclusion was that the area's "testing ground for black-white integration" had failed. But the numbers tell a different story. When Southfield was hailed as a shining example of integration in 1990, it was 68 percent white and 29 percent Black. In 2000, the suburb was 39 percent white and 54 percent Black, and those figures were considered proof that integration had failed.[9] The difference is that whenever the scales tip to a Black majority, the tendency is to consider it a sea of Blackness.

It is a no-win situation, so why not congregate? Even kids in my third-grade class knew there was strength in numbers. That is what the Black lunch table is all about. It is a safe zone where all eyes will not be on you because now you are the pack and not the Only. For the current crop of young Black executives, there are no drawbacks to congregating. There is no reason to hide who they are because those that came before them already tried that and it didn't work—that's why there are so few Black CEOs.

Working While Black is disturbing because the consequences are much greater than the inconvenience of being pulled over on I-95. We spend at least eight hours of our day, a significant chunk of our lives, at work. It is often more time than we spend with our families. That is just too long a period for anyone to be trapped in a While Black cage.

Susan Chapman is a 34-year-old senior finance executive and director of global real estate for Level 3, a major technology company. At her company's Denver headquarters, she is also the ambassador of Black America. "They don't know anything about Susan, about my life. But I am the only Black person they know so of course I speak for all Black America." You can count the number of Black executives at Susan's company on one hand. But her complaints about representing a mass of Blackness and the isolation that it stirs up are far from unique. Susan's frustration is hard to forget. It is like its own WWB e-mail waiting to be FWD.

Number one on Susan's list is the comfort of ignorance. Let's call it the art of just "not getting it." Alone in Colorado,

Susan works for a company with a CEO named James Crowe, who prefers to be called Jim. Really. One day, during a company retreat, Susan made up a Level 3 edition of Jeopardy for her staff to help them work together as a team. Her best Alex Trebek impression was a hit and everything was going well. Then came the question that stumped the room. It was under the topic of "Senior Management." The $200 clue: "His name is synonymous with a major civil rights faux pas." The room of 30 was silent. That day the cage was crushing for Susan, the ambassador. "How could none of them not have made that connection before? I will never understand that," she fumed. The connection being, of course, that the name of their company's CEO was also the name of a major part of civil rights history. As in, Who is Jim Crow(e)?

It sounds minor. But the isolation, pressure, and frustration that these executives feel cannot be overestimated. Every Black executive I talked to had stories of being the "Only." Talk of "they" peppers conversation constantly, and "versus me" eventually becomes understood. "Do they notice?" one 34-year-old marketing VP asked desperately. "Do they look around the room like I do and think, 'Wow, there's only one Black guy here'?" A big part of the isolation is the barrage of insensitivity, subtle and not so, that inevitably results from being the Only or one of a few. It doesn't mean that the masses are intentionally trying to single out the few. But eventually it will happen. The mass exists because there are things that tie it together and exclude others. At the end of a long day, it is a recipe for disaster if you are one of the few. As in, Who is Jim Crow(e)!

The harder part is actually being just one of only a few. Although the ranks of Black executives continue to increase with each generation (even *Fortune* magazine now ranks the Top 50 African Americans in Business), the successes are still very much sprinkled. So every company (and some more than others) has just a few successful Black faces.

For young Black professionals (the current crop of 30-something execs who are scrambling up the corporate ladder now), this can be a heavy burden. These post-civil rights executives can see, even in the neighborhoods they live in, the critical mass of Black success. It is a mass that collectively holds significant power. Unlike the previous generation, they know they are not the only ones out there who have climbed so high. They have been to the same B-schools, law schools, and the best prep schools together. Socially, they can—and often do—exist in an all-encompassing world of Black elite. There are Black vice presidents, executive vice presidents, general managers, managing directors, and partners. Prestigious, big-wig sounding titles that can be splashed across a business card are common and, more importantly, are expected. So, to come into the office on Monday morning and be the Only generates more than feelings of isolation. It seems hostile and oppressive. In their minds, there is no reason the office still has to look like that. With their eyes always on the collective mass of Black professionals, the lack of representation, then, couldn't have just happened. The fact that the office looks that way becomes proof of something that is being done deliberately. Therefore, it must be reacted to, deliberately. The responses can range from one's own hostile action to the constant need to always fight back. On Monday in the office, these young Black professionals don't back down. They are not afraid to speak up because they feel they have nothing to lose. They organize and support each other and are always prepared to leave—the situation, the company, the system even—if need be. In Susan's case, she did not remain silent after the Jeopardy game. Her frustration was clear to anyone in the room. "I felt like a history teacher," she says. Susan also did not let the

Jim Crow(e) connection drop there, but brought it up again in passing whenever she got the chance, so her staff could not forget the sheltered bubble that they had once comfortably existed in. Not getting it—at least about Jim Crow—could not be an excuse.

Working While Black

7. You continually get more responsibility, but no authority.
16. You are told your attitude is affecting others. You are asked to . . . "lighten up, not be so serious about the work. Smile and laugh more often, to make others more comfortable working with you."
18. You have to perform at 250 percent just to stay even.
19. You have to document everything. You've learned the hard way.

Alvin Bowles, 29, is the best kind of executive—never satisfied. Hailing from the suburbs of the nation's most segregated city—Detroit—Alvin was bred on prep school, the University of Michigan, and Harvard Business School. He spent three years as an investment banker at J.P. Morgan before moving over to the music industry, where he is an executive at Sony. He has moved steadily up the ladder and is now in charge of brokering commercial partnerships and endorsement deals between artists and corporate America. But Alvin tells it like this: "I am the most senior Black person in strategic marketing at Sony Music and I am a director—which is bullshit!" We were sitting in Alvin's midtown Manhattan office one spring afternoon. For the music industry, it had that very corporate *I've arrived* cache—large windows, plush carpet, a master-of-the-universe desk. At the time, Alvin was juggling a $30 million account with Pepsi—a major venture for Sony—and the campaign's first television ads were just starting to hit the airways.

By corporate standards, he is doing well, even if in terms of Black progress it is still bull.

Married with a kid on the way, Alvin works—all the time. He always has either a call to take or a meeting to attend, whether it is for his job at Sony, his service as a volunteer mentor to Black teenagers, or his political fund-raising activities. (He collects hundreds of thousands of dollars for local Democratic candidates to make sure the Black vote is heard.) His phone rings constantly as we sit in his office. Most of all, he works at being a successful Black man, keeping the community at large in mind first by committing the best thing he can, himself. At Sony, that means being the best because his is the only Black face. "I feel the weight of that burden," he says. "I feel my work being scrutinized. I am clearly an African American male and unapologetically Black. So it is not just enough to get the right answer. I am going to have to do it faster and quicker and better." As he says this at work late one evening, the surrounding offices are all already empty for the night. He walks me through the darkened hall to the elevator and turns back to his office. There is still work to do.

Alvin touches on something that is intrinsic to WWB— twice as good, as in, you have to be twice as good for the same reward if you're Black. "Twice as good" is **not** new. It is the motto in any Black household concerned with success. Ask Black standouts in any field and it will come up. "If you want to be successful, you have to outwork the other guy," Dick Parsons, CEO of Time Warner, advises me. "I never thought I would make it without working the hardest in the room." This is what Black parents teach their children and what children learn from their parents. It is a part of what it means to be Black in the United States. And trying to be twice as good all the time is exhausting.

Although the twice-as-good credo is not unique to the 30-something set, never before has the issue of being overlooked been so pronounced. Thanks to the civil rights movement, affirmative action, hard work, and progress, this group is the most privileged of any generation of African Americans. On paper, they look the same as, or better than, their white counterparts. They have the degrees and the experience going in. So, there is a healthy sense of entitlement. They expect their credentials will be rewarded. Simply, "I expect to win," says Alvin. When they don't win, resentment builds. So, it is not surprising that the harshest zingers of the WWB e-mail related to not being recognized. With each Fwd, these items got the most comment, support, and amens. It is a signal of just how serious the disconnect is and how much farther we still need to go.

Back at the Black table in the cafeteria, there is a lot of talk about getting what is owed. These are not 40 acres-and-a-mule fantasies. It is about legitimate frustration when the story does not end the same way for them as it does for their white colleagues: I did this, I did this, I did this, but I still didn't get the promotion. At the office of one media company, they call it the "jet pack" phenomenon—the inexplicable rapid shot up the corporate ladder that some *other* people always seem to get. This is a world of "golden boys" and everyone else. The golden boys are usually unremarkable in every way except that they get everything handed to them. Each promotion of the golden boy provides additional proof that the jet pack phenomenon is in effect. The golden boy is the person in the office who manages to capture every opportunity to succeed, every plum assignment, while the rest must fight for themselves. The golden boy is also never Black. Sometimes the favoritism is blatant— lunches during the week, invites on the weekends. Other times, behavior might be subtler, but in the end these Black professionals still have an overwhelming sense that they are somehow being left out. When Sean concluded that metrics vary for different people, it was precisely after watching his company's most senior Black executive pitted against a golden boy for a promotion.

Anyone working in a competitive environment gets hit with feelings of being undervalued and unappreciated now and then. But not everyone can point to race as the reason. These days you can change almost anything about yourself if you think it will help you succeed. You can even change your sex if that is what it is going to take to be happy. But your race is the one characteristic that no one can ever change (even Michael Jackson). Which makes talk like I did this, I did this, I did this, but I still didn't get the promotion, hard to ignore.

We are traveling down a slippery slope here, I know. This is squarely territory where those who get it need no convincing, and those who don't will never be convinced. Racism is like that. It is one of those emotion-filled crimes where it is often hard to obtain evidence. How can you prove that your dignity has been hit? How do you convince someone that you have been slighted? Where is the line of disrespect? Still, no matter how fluctuating these questions may seem, there is never any doubt when you are the victim. And, thus, the crime only gets worse when people don't believe that it has happened.

Remember those federal findings about the hard-core discrimination that African Americans go through in the workplace? All the statistics were troubling, but the one that really stood out for me was that 10 percent of the nation's companies practice the highest level of employment discrimination recognized by government and have been doing so for more than 10 years.[10] That is hard core. Thirty years ago, such findings would have been expected and thus easier to accept. But today, when things supposedly have changed for the better, the reality can be disheartening. It is at the heart of why younger Black executives refuse to apologize for their Blackness.

Oral Muir, a 33-year-old e-commerce executive for Marriott, has a knack for offering nuggets of profound ideas no matter how short the conversation (my favorite is the quote that started this chapter). Oral is a native of Jamaica and moved to New York City when he was 12. He hasn't been back to the island since. But, living his formative years in a country where Black is the majority, with power and leaders, has profoundly shaped his outlook on what is possible. The experience helped instill in him a deep sense of pride and filled his head with the knowledge that there are unlimited opportunities for Black people. In Jamaica, Black did not mean disenfranchised minority, but the exact opposite. He expects Black people to be leaders because he has experienced that world. Most of all, he says, seeing Black on top for 12 years gave him a sense of power. "I experienced being a winner," he says. "You never lose that." It is something he wishes that every Black face in the United States could experience.

Like many of his generation, Oral has no patience for Black executives who are timid with their Blackness in the office. In part, it reflects the sense of isolation and marginalization that this generation feels. These highly educated overachievers find themselves fighting just as much for recognition and opportunity as the groundbreakers did. And if you are still fighting anyway, then why not be completely honest? In this realistic view, race is something then that cannot and will not be hidden. With no hope of actually changing the hurdles, they instead expect to succeed despite them. That is a key difference of this generation. For the first time, a generation is willing to look away from the inequalities and mistreatment at large. By admitting that they don't have the power to change things and make the field level, they are driven to succeed completely on their own terms. That is why Oral doesn't believe in playing the role of the raceless wonder just to make others feel comfortable.

"People are screwed up," he says matter-of-factly. "Folks are always going to hate each other. That's why masks don't make any sense."

This generation talks a lot about masks. It is often the mask, perceived or not, that others wear in the office to survive being Black in corporate America. As Black executives, how much of themselves do they hide and how much do they allow to surface? They accuse those who came before of walking on eggshells when dealing with issues of race. One of seven, Sean, broke it down this way: The generation of groundbreakers wears opaque masks. His generation's masks are translucent. And he hopes that by the time his newborn son goes to work, the mask will be transparent.

For Oral, part of destroying the mask is being the constant voice of race in the office. "If I don't bring up these issues, then who will?" he asks. That has not always been the cry from Black executives in the office just trying to secure their place. More often, the advice has been to choose your battles. But for professionals of this generation, who are a little shell-shocked by just how hard things are, everything is a battle.

In his first corporate job as a technology consultant at a boutique firm, Oral noticed one summer that two young Black students were roaming the office without any direction or guidance. He concluded that they were interns stuck in a minority program with expectations set too low. One day when the firm's CEO made an appearance on the staff floor for a meet-and-greet session, Oral had only one question during the brief encounter, which was not really meant for questions: "What's up with the two Black kids?" His unexpected directness caught the CEO off guard and caused murmurs around the office. Oral, however, has no regrets for always speaking directly about race. Because of his candor, the CEO asked him to create and lead the firm's nonprofit arm, which eventually acted as a liaison between Fortune 500 companies and urban neighborhoods. The division created yearlong internships and weekend workshops for as many as 300 students. Oral's goal? Give concrete experience so no one else could ask, "What's up with the Black kids in the office?" He also served as a consultant to other firms that wanted to create similar endeavors. Being honest about race helped Oral create opportunity and succeed, and prevented him from compromising on what he really wanted to do. When he was ready to leave the company, the CEO acted as a mentor, helping him field offers and eventually decide on Marriott. For today's young Black executives, such honesty about race is the only plan that works.

The danger with chitchat of golden boys and jet packs is that it will always leave people at the table dissatisfied. The bottom line is that as long as Black executives are not seen leading the pack, these feelings of frustration and resentment will continue to ferment. The Fortune 500 has four Black CEOs. Whereas the previous generation, with memories of no access, celebrates the achievement as amazing progress, the post-civil rights babies see *only* four. For a generation that has never lived in a world where they are not even let inside the door, leading the pack is what matters most. Alvin thinks his position at Sony is "bullshit," not because he isn't proud of his success, but because he feels he has not climbed high enough on the corporate ladder to be the highest ranking Black face in strategic marketing. There should be someone who has climbed higher. Sean is disturbed that he is one of seven, but he is downright disgusted that none of those seven were at a high enough level to be on the stage at the company meeting.

Who cares if folks gripe at lunchtime? Really. These are not, however, just any group of gripers. The current crop of

Black professionals represents the success of the civil rights movement. This is what all the fighting was for–to make this group possible. And they are still complaining about race. That is why we should care.

My favorite item on the WWB countdown was the last:

Working While Black

20. You presumed that all that was required of you was to work hard and get the job done.

I could have uttered these words myself. I *have* uttered these words myself. It is the feeling that nothing is ever enough. It will never be enough because the rules of success have changed, again. One of the distinctions between the current group of black professionals and the previous generation is that 30-somethings are cynical. Sean steamrollering toward his 32- or 34-day finish line called the equality promises a "fairy tale." Such cynicism comes from the moment in time that this generation blossomed–blame it on the 1980s. It comes from watching their parents do everything necessary and still not become leaders. It comes from trying to survive isolation. It comes from unexpected insensitivity hurled out of (turtlenecked) corners once thought to be friendly. And it comes from those changing rules. The mere fact that this generation has achieved success by standing on the shoulders of those who died to make it happen, is a breeding ground for cynicism when that success is not considered enough. It also comes from having faith that things were supposed to be different. Hence, the jokes and the WWB countdown. Number 20 represents that little bit of faith beginning to break.

Coincidentally, at the end of that Working While Black e-mail I got that day in my inbox was a quote by Harriet Tubman:

If I could have convinced more slaves that they were slaves, I could have freed thousands more.

It is a quote that we've all seen dozens of times during Black History month, as a tag line on Afrocentric calendars, T-shirts, and paperweights in Black bookstores. Familiarity and cheesy consumerism make it is easy to overlook the insight those words hold. But, alongside the twentieth item on the WWB list, the power of Tubman's point was blinding.

Seeing her words in my inbox that day, I smiled. This time it was a Kool-Aid grin moment.

2

BEYOND RAGE

There clearly is a heavyweight set of African Americans in business now. It is time we leverage that.
—Richard Gay, 35, partner, Booz Allen Hamilton

*T*his generation of Black executives is not knocking down doors, shattering concrete ceilings, or becoming "the Firsts." Their parents did that. It was their parents who also discovered that climbing to the top often came with a lot of frustration that author Ellis Cose dubbed "the Rage" a decade ago in his book *The Rage of a Privileged Class*. Yes, despite their success, Black professionals were angry. Life wasn't as good as they thought it would be. Racism has a way of screwing that up. There were still doors that they couldn't open, gaps that wouldn't close, and hurdles that they couldn't jump. They were Black doctors, Black lawyers, Black corporate vice presidents, and Black journalists, . . . and Black. First and foremost, they were still seen as Black, and they were not getting the respect that they deserved. The current crop of Black executives may not have knocked down many doors, but they were raised with the frustration of those who had.

Cose depicts the rage of successful middle-class Black professionals in vivid, unforgettable detail. An insurance VP who had trouble joining a country club expressed his rage by testifying about it before the U.S. Senate Judiciary Committee. A two-star army general recounted how he was constantly forced to show additional ID when entering his base in Biloxi, Mississippi—such disrespect leaps from the page. And who could forget the big city police detective who was viciously brutalized by a group of fellow cops, all white, when he was working undercover? He needed surgery to close the wounds. Still, after he was stitched up, he said nothing to his superiors about the incident—silence was very much a part of how that generation of Black professionals succeeded—but he was angry. By the time the detective crossed paths with Cose, he was worried that someday he would lose control and all his anger would just come spewing out.

Cose also tells the story of a corporate attorney who was forced to play chicken early one morning with a young white attorney who insisted on physically blocking the Black man's path to the office door until he produced his identification. The Black man was a partner at the firm behind the door and the white man was a young associate, but that hadn't mattered. As I read about the lawyer pouring his heart out about his anger, ticking off all the things on his résumé that had gotten him to where he was, one detail stood out for me. "He and his wife were in the process of raising three exemplary children."[1] We are now in the age of those "three exemplary children."

The frustration and rage have not gone away. The post-civil rights generation, though, is no longer surprised when rage comes; as a result, these professionals are able to move beyond it. They don't let frustration cripple them as it did the generation before. They use the rage and frustration as motivators. I am a Black journalist, not a journalist who happens to be Black. *There is a difference.* My goal is to bring that perspective to the news and deliver news from that perspective. On some idealistic level, I think this helps all African Americans. Likewise, Black executives of this generation want to achieve because they are Black. Thus, their measure of success has changed. Success for the post-civil rights generation is directly tied to what it means for Black folks. They are looking for roles, positions, and status that will bring value for a group of people still undervalued. They measure success by the influence, wealth, and knowledge that they can bring to the group. They have embraced the business world because they see it as the best venue in which to achieve that kind of Black success. That is what matters.

We are all a reflection of our parents. Sometimes we embrace their characteristics; other times we do our Alex P. Keaton best to be the opposite. My mom is anally neat and has even managed to reduce the lives of me and my brother to a color-coded filing system in her bedroom that would make any office manager proud. I am much more relaxed when it comes to putting things away, so much so that several years ago the local fire marshal declared my paper-cluttered desk was a fire hazard during a routine inspection of the newsroom. Under the watchful eye of the newspaper's executives, I was forced to clean until I could see the Formica.

Sometimes, though, we embrace and improve, or adapt. My brother has taken the anal neatness gene to a whole new level of unprecedented efficiency. This generation is like my brother—in this third category. They are taking things another step forward. After watching their parents' rage, frustration is, expected. They are mindful of the environment that created such disappointment; they can't ignore it. They cling so strongly to the "race-matters" motto because the frustration they were raised with taught them that the motto holds true. Yes, they expect the door to be open because they have already seen Black faces pass through. But they don't expect to play the game on a level field once they are inside. They don't expect to fit in or to feel especially accepted. The world is better, but just slightly.

For proof, listen to Wishart Edwards, a 34-year-old investment banker. "Like it or not, race guides everything we do. That is the way it is," he says with such matter-of-fact force that as a listener you have no choice but to nod your head in agreement. Wishart is an executive director (partner) at UBS, the Swiss bank. On the verge of becoming a partner at Morgan Stanley, he stunned colleagues when he bolted for the Swiss firm. He made the move because he felt a foreign company would offer better opportunities for African Americans. "At the end of the day you are always going to be a Black person trying to get something that no one wants to give you." I nod my head in agreement.

Wishart likens the workplace for Black executives to judo. As a journalist covering business, I hear a lot of sports analogies. But martial arts was a new one. I learned, though, that judo is all about anticipating movements. The point is to move so adeptly that you avoid the blows you know are surely coming. Likewise, this generation knows generally what to expect. So, rage is now a part of Black success. It comes with the territory. No matter how much young Black executives may kick and scream that it is unfair, not a single one who talked with me expected things to change in any significant way. According to the Joint Center for Politics and Economics, 81 percent of Black professionals think workplace discrimination is still common.[2] This is not merely the belief that job discrimination exists, but that it is *common*. The judo way is just not to be there when the racist blows arrive.

Because this frustration is now expected, the post-civil rights generation is turning rage into action. This is the adaptation and improvement part of development. It is crazy to do exactly what their parents did, only to end up frustrated. But, it is also close to impossible to avoid frustration when still faced with the same triggers. IDs of Black professionals are still being checked in corporate hallways. To survive, the only choice, then, is to *use* that unavoidable frustration. Otherwise, those who don't adapt will be destroyed, or at least stalled in their advancement, which for some can be the same as destruction. So this generation, aware of the rage, is not trying to get rid of it. But they do not let it control them either. Instead, they know that they must control it and use it to their advantage. If this generation can manage that, they win.

So, Black executives, armed with better degrees, résumés, and professional networks than any that came before, are moving Beyond Rage to action. They are using the benefits of integration to move on and do something for their own. This is significant. This is their movement. Black and Proud(er) is the chant in the office. Having a party? Thanks for the invite, but we're throwing our own!

In the meantime, they are changing the rules. That is their action.

That is why Oral Muir, the IT consultant, did not blink an eye when he boldly asked his company's CEO "what [was] up with the two Black kids in the office." Dell Vice President Kim Goodman doesn't feel the need to keep secret her ultimate goal: uplifting the Black community, and one day starting her own business to fulfill that goal. It is something she told Michael Dell when he hired her and something she continues to discuss openly in the office with anyone who will listen. Susan Chapman, the "ambassador" in Colorado, stunned her superiors when she turned down a new position that they offered her. "They aren't used to people telling them no," she said. "In their mind it was an opportunity. It would have helped me within this company. But it would have done nothing to move me closer to the goals that I want to accomplish [for Black America]." This is not the typical corporate talk. And it is certainly not what you would hear from those concerned with becoming firsts just for the sake of being first. The measure of success has shifted for this group. "It is painful to break through glass ceilings," says Erica Dukes, 34, of J.P. Morgan. "It doesn't always add value either."

Erica used to work on a trading floor. It is just as you've seen in the movies. When stocks are being actively traded, it's total pandemonium, with hundreds of people waving their arms and shouting to do the right transaction at precisely the right moment. The goal is always the same: Make money. Perhaps more than any other workplace, trading floors are vast white seas of testosterone. One former trader teared up reliving the day she accidentally dropped a tampon in the middle of the floor on her way to the restroom. "Watch out guys," someone howled from the floor. "PMS coming through." It was junior high all over again. Another remembered when a fellow trader brought his young son to the floor. Immediately, he began crying. The frightened child looked through that sea of hundreds and ran straight to her for comfort. "No one really knew what was going on," she says. "I did. I was the only Black woman in the room. He thought I was the nanny." So Erica moved over to investment banking where she now regularly pulls all-nighters to get deals done. The locker room is more civilized—the members play golf instead of quarters, but Erica, still the only Black female face, is not yet convinced that it's worth it. "I just don't see how I add value at this point. I just don't see it."

Perhaps the most profound way this generation changes the rules is by refusing to deny who they are—young, Black, and proud. This influences their choices, their outlook, and their priorities. It is one of the strongest actions these executives can make. The strength that comes from never giving up an ounce of who they are may sound subtle, even insignificant. But for a population that has been forced to give itself up since being brought to these shores, to stand proud and never compromise their identity is nothing less than empowering. To dare to say "take it or leave it" is radical. To value self first is forceful. This is what the post-civil rights generation is doing. If the groundbreaker generation can be characterized as doing what they had to do to succeed within a system already in place, this generation is trying to succeed despite the system. They don't see any reason to sacrifice themselves to succeed. Unconsciously perhaps, they prefer not climbing as high if it means they might have to compromise a part of their Blackness.

"As an African American man, I needed a place I could be an individual," says Richard Gay, talking about how he became a media and entertainment consultant with Booz Allen. This was one of his chief concerns when looking for a career and deciding on a firm. "Wall Street has a strong culture. A lot of other consulting firms had a strong culture. I'm sure I could have done that and succeeded—but I'm not sure that I wanted to. I didn't want to conform. I wanted to be an individual. That was more important for me."

Richard is proof that take-it-or-leave-it can work. He made partner at the blue-chip consulting firm at 32. Although he found a firm where he's comfortable, the consulting industry is anything but diverse. It is a clubby world of Ivy League golden boys that is difficult for outsiders to penetrate. Making partner takes years of long hours and hard work, and often involves mastering a political process in which contacts and alliances can matter as much as merit. Private firms dominate the industry, and information about it is hard to come by. Consultants are great at dishing out advice and the goods on other businesses, but they reveal little about themselves. For a recent article in *Consulting Magazine,* the industry's own cheerleader publication, not one of the top 10 firms would disclose the number of minority partners in its ranks. The magazine concluded that the lack of diversity in the industry was so severe that it probably hadn't improved much from a decade earlier when the number of Black partners at top firms could be counted on two hands.[3] So Richard's success is a big deal.

He wears his status well. A BS from Wharton, an MBA from Stanford, and an I-Belong attitude help. Charming, confident, and comfortable, the only sign that he's still climbing the ladder is that he hasn't yet moved his things into one of the big offices usually handed to partners. "Soon, soon," he insists. At 35, Richard is the youngest of the Black partners at Booz Allen. The firm is considered a diversity success story in the industry because of its 150 partners, 5 are Black. Despite his conservative clean-shaven corporate environment, Richard typically sports a goatee or even a beard. He also heads the firm's African American Core Team, a company committee dedicated to Black recruitment, retention, and advancement at the firm. He's the poster child for succeeding without compromising.

Midway through our conversation on hopes and dreams and Working While Black anecdotes, Richard started to get serious. "For this generation it would be so easy to just be successful," he declares. "Not easy to *be* successful. But easy to just focus on being successful. If you want to have a great job and be rich and live up in Westchester you can do that." Richard, by the way, has a great job, makes a good salary, and lives in Westchester County, an elite suburban area near New York City. "The challenge is recognizing the impact that we *can* have. And I would argue we *should* have. It is our obligation."

While growing up in the suburbs of Chicago, Richard's family encouraged him to join the ministry. When he gets serious, you can see why—his talk is inspiring. That impact is why Richard went into corporate America. Impact governs his choices and influences his decisions in the workplace and gets him through any frustration. It informs the action that he takes and the legacy he is trying to leave for those that follow. As much as Richard likes being a consultant for a top-notch firm— and he admittedly likes it a lot (he even gets excited about cranking out analyses at his computer)—his career is still very much a means to an end. And that end is impact. He is rising through the ranks not only for himself but for those Black faces to follow because with success comes influence, which is what's important to Richard and his peers. As a partner, Richard feels he has a platform to speak as something larger than himself and has access to funds that can make a difference. This is what matters. This, as he says, is his obligation.

"We are getting in the positions to do it." *It,* of course, being impact again. "I used to do things on an individual level—Big Brother programs, mentoring. Now, as a partner at Booz Allen I control some resources. I can do pro bono work and sell work to clients I want to sell to. I can donate some of my funds and more importantly some of Booz Allen's funds to causes I think make a difference. I now try to find a way to have an institutional impact. How can I make sure that Booz Allen, as an institution, has an impact making things better for African Americans."

Such conviction coincides with the wave of economic empowerment that is now gripping Black America. It is not surprising that Richard's family would push him toward the church. In past generations, someone like Richard, so concerned with uplifting the race, indeed would have come from the ministry. But instead of the church, or even politics, this generation has turned to business to have the greatest impact. By the mid-1990s, Black empowerment had become synonymous with economics. Surveys were starting to show that by a wide margin (50 percent versus 31 percent) Black professionals would like to see Black leaders focus their attention on business instead of politics.[4] The previous year, Hugh Price, then President of the National Urban League, sat down for an interview with *Fortune* magazine. The theme of the civil rights organization's annual convention that summer was Economic Power: The Next Civil Rights Frontier. The magazine, in turn, decided to devote an issue to what it dubbed the "New Black

Power," shining a spotlight on the groundswell of Black clout in business that was just starting to gather force.

"It's an important time for our country," Price told *Fortune*. "Just as the nation is implementing rollbacks to the efforts designed to create equal opportunities for all Americans, the generation of African Americans who benefited most from those programs is beginning to take its place at the table of economic success."[5] Not wanting to be left behind, that same year Jesse Jackson created the Wall Street Project to monitor corporate America and started popping up at annual shareholder meetings, using the forum to bring up issues of race. The Wall Street Project managed to get the stock exchange to shut down in observance of Martin Luther King Jr.'s birthday. The organization's annual conference now attracts some of the biggest names in business.

This generation is coming of age in the midst of that economic sphere. Their climb up the corporate ladder is fueled by their desire to have an impact. Instead of marching for voting rights and desegregation, they are concerned with building Black wealth. The power and influence will come with that.

These days, it makes sense to equate economics with power. We are, after all, in an age when our president has an MBA, not a JD, and has chosen to surround himself with corporate executives. At one point, four cabinet members and the chief of staff of the current Bush administration were all former CEOs. Vice President Cheney was CEO of Halliburton, an oil services company, while Defense Secretary Donald Rumsfeld donned the CEO hat twice, first at pharmaceutical company GD Searle in the 1970s and then at General Instruments, now part of Motorola. Bush plucked Commerce Secretary Don Evans from the top spot at Tom Brown Energy, an oil and gas enterprise; and former Treasury Secretary Paul O'Neil used to be the chief of Alcoa, the aluminum giant. No president since Eisenhower has had more than one ex-CEO in his cabinet, and Eisenhower had only two. Other corporate power brokers included Army Secretary Tom White, former head of the energy-trading arm at Enron; and Air Force Secretary James Roche and Navy Secretary Gordon England, who both came from military technology companies, Northrup Grumman and General Dynamics, respectively.

Among Black professionals, the economics mantra has become such a given that it is hard not to hear such talk at dinner parties, college reunions, and at the Black table in the cafeteria. A friend once tried to challenge me on this sweeping generalization. How could I possibly just assume that our generation looks to business as the answer? How could I not? Some things are so pervasive that all you can do is make sweeping generalizations. It is like saying white middle-class college kids in the 1960s were against the war in Vietnam or that Fidel Castro wouldn't be welcomed in Miami. It's that obvious; that's just the way it is. Back in 1997, Biggie rapped about "Flossin' on the cover of *Fortune*" as the epitome of success, and no one blinked, because for this generation it is all about economics. So, yes, there are lots out there, like Richard, who are embracing business as their movement.

"I actually believe money goes a long way in making a difference in the United States of America," says Richard. The son of a teacher of disabled children and of a nuclear scientist ("my Dad holds patents," he gushes with pride), Richard went off to Wharton when he was 18 precisely because he felt business could have the biggest impact. "It may sound crass to say money makes a difference but I fundamentally believe that. In politics, you have to go through too much to make a change. In business, whether it is my personal funds, or the funds I control, or the people I know who control a lot more funds than me, we can make things happen pretty quickly if we want to."

There are exceptions in any generalization. Ironically, the people closest in Richard's life are not in business. His best friend is a civil rights attorney in Los Angeles whom Richard constantly teases for trying to make change one case at a time. "He may set a precedent that might matter 20 years from now," Richard shrugs. His older brother is a surgeon who "saves lives in the inner city." His wife, Cynthia, is currently in graduate school getting her PhD in education. "They are all going to save the world and that is great," Richard says. "But, when they need the money to do it, I'll be here."

That type of confidence can be intoxicating. This generation has the focus and the drive. It has mastered the one-for-all doctrine. They are convinced they can make their dreams come true, *their* way.* Despite all that, the inherent frustrations that come with climbing higher still remain. Even if they are not the Firsts, this generation of Black executives is still most likely the Onlys. And that's no picnic either. Working While Black, baggage, discrimination (Richard calls it "the noise")—none of it has gone away.

"I don't want to paint a story that race doesn't matter, because it does," Richard says over and over as we talk about big hopes and big dreams. "What else do I need to do? I went to the schools I went to. Progressed as I should at Booz Allen. What else do I need to do to get rid of this noise and not have to deal with this?"

Feel it? This is the rage.

But then Richard moves Beyond Rage. He quickly adds: "I say that not really in seriousness because I know I'll always have to deal with it [the noise]. We can be Black doctors, Black lawyers, Black businessmen, but we are still Black first and all those other things follow. It is just a fact. So you better get

---

*If you caught this *Laverne & Shirley* reference, then you also spent too much of the 1970s in front of the tube. For the rest of you, one day listen to the sitcom's theme song past Schlemeel, Schlemazel.

comfortable in that situation if you want to be successful in any industry and figure out how you are going to deal with that."

Richard is not expecting that noise to change. It might be a part of that WWB cynicism or part of the armor this generation needs to survive. It might be nothing more than simply being realistic. It doesn't really matter. If nothing is going to change, the challenge becomes what you can get, despite such noise.

And that's the interesting part.

Moving Beyond Rage is what this generation is all about. That doesn't mean the rage no longer exists. Remember Richard's plea: "What else do I need to do?" The exasperation is deafening. The rage still exists, but this generation is not trying to change the world. They are trying to succeed despite the world. Richard ends his comments with the implicit command to figure out how to "deal with that."

So "moving beyond" has become not only what ties this generation together but what sets it apart from those that came before. The rage is no longer a debilitating weakness. Instead, the ability to move beyond is the post-civil rights generation's most powerful asset. They have a focus that others cannot sway or discourage. "The instant I feel my mind moving to victim—even if I am the victim—I've lost," says Kim at Dell. "It doesn't do me any good." Without the higher purpose, the rage wins. The Black attorney that Ellis Cose wrote about had become so angry after a white associate blocked his way and demanded his ID that it was all he could think about. "Because of his color, he felt he had the right to check me out," hisses the Black lawyer. Cose concludes that it was an ongoing source of "immense resentment."[6] By wasting that much energy on rage, he could not possibly be fulfilling his success potential. Because Black professionals in this new wave expect to be checked out, they have an advantage: They're ready.

If such focus holds true, it would make sense that the post-civil rights generation would be harder to knock down than even the one that came before. Aren't children supposed to grow up to be tougher and stronger? That is what happens when you have the advantage of adopting all your parents' strengths and improving on their weaknesses. Alvin, the Sony music executive, gets right to the point: "We've done all these things because we are standing on someone else's blood, sweat, and tears. Literally." Sometimes this generation forgets how much it owes to the past, even if it is just seeing a model of how they don't want to do things today. "It is easy to look smart when you are standing on the shoulders of geniuses," says Alvin. "I am standing on the shoulders of someone who blazed the trail for me and I look a hell of a lot better because of it." So if we are truly moving forward, then the current generation has to be a little bit stronger.

Also, if you always expect the noise, the rage, the hurdles, your goals can't help but change. For this generation, the change occurs without lowering their standards or settling for less. Instead, they focus on what matters most to them and that is usually being Black. Because they know the noise does not go away, race has become even more important. Richard thinks that, by becoming a partner, his access to resources can make things better for all African Americans; Kim, the VP from Dell, wants to start a business to give African Americans access to capital. These are just as idealistic as the civil rights goal of racial equality was before them, but cynicism has been thrown in. They don't want to change the world, they want to change just the world that matters to them—the Black one. As a result, race becomes not only the motivator but the reason for being.

It is almost like living a double life. These young executives are focusing on what they can take and use from the 9-to-5. So, yes, they are using lunch hours to plan a revolution. Everything they learn is filtered through the lunchtime lens as well. This generation is constantly thinking about what they will need to do something else—that is the blueprint, or rather the *Blackprint,* they follow. These Black executives are paying attention to everything and making decisions based on what is good for them, not necessarily what is expected of them (even from the company). They don't live for the fulfillment of someone else's dream (or company); they are intent on fulfilling their own dreams. They are interested in paths where they can learn. The intention is always that the post-civil rights generation will use what they learn here in some other capacity there and for themselves: Again, that's the Blackprint. Of course, their white counterparts may be dreaming bigger dreams, too. But those white counterparts also have the luxury of focusing only on what it takes to uplift themselves, not an entire race.

Talk of double lives, Blackprints, and alternative intentions is sure to make some people (read: bosses, managers, even parents) nervous. But the post-civil rights babies are still holding it down in the office. We are talking about a group of overachievers, the largest generation of successful Black professionals to date. This group will no doubt be able to soar higher than those who came before. So the revolution cannot hamper performance. Being able to do both well is the meaning of Black success. This generation still tends to succeed. Splitting their focus prevents the rage from destroying them. It is freeing to know that there is more beyond that ladder. They feel empowered to say what they want to say and do what they want to do. This is the difference between wanting to be invited to the party and wanting to throw the party. When you throw the party, you tailor it to your needs, whatever they might be. You can do whatever you want, even cry—it's your party. (Sorry, I couldn't resist.) But when someone else throws the party and wants you to be there, it means that at some level you are accepted and liked—hence the invitation. No one has to like you if you want to throw a party; it may not be successful, but you can still throw it.

"My goal is to get to the point where I am running things," says Richard, nonchalantly. Just as Alvin of Sony declares: "I expect to win," and Susan, the ambassador in Colorado, wants to "be the one on top." The desire is to be in charge, and the prizes are power, influence, and control. Richard did not say he wants to run things at Booz Allen or even another consulting firm. The emphasis was on running things, period. The parents of this generation wanted to go as far as they could go, but assumed they would never run things. This generation, itself, wants to be in charge. There is a difference. Getting to the top of the ladder is no longer the reward; it is just necessary to fulfill these dreams of power. It is what you do at the top that matters, specifically what you do for Black folks, that is the measure of success. Without sounding too abstract, the action that these executives are taking redefines the very meaning of success. That is also how Beyond Rage can work, because the concept of success has shifted: For this generation, success is no longer dependent on systems beyond their control.

There is still, for the lack of a better word, the bad. "Race still matters" plays like a broken record in all these conversations. It is this generation's theme song at the office. They still hear "the noise." Life isn't quiet yet, but the bad is less debilitating because the focus has shifted.

That is what Beyond Rage is all about—using advantages and pushing limits, because now there are no excuses. They know what the hardships will be, and they're ready. The Richards, Kims, Orals, Ericas, and Alvins are not so much concerned with gaining access, in part because they assume access. But they do expect access to be limited at some point. So instead of focusing on gaining access, they are more concerned with *using* it. "It doesn't matter how hard I work, at some point I am going to be marginalized," says Sean, at BMS, with WWB memories still fresh. "So I'm constantly looking and thinking about the next move because I am not doing any of this not to have some influence."

Which brings us back to the younger set's preoccupation with the business world. Sean's assessment of corporate America was that it is not a meritocracy. At this point, with government studies of hard-core discrimination, it is hard to argue with that characterization. Among Black professionals, 81 percent (the percentage who think discrimination is common) agree with Sean. Yet, business is the one institution that has the best chance of ever becoming a meritocracy. If the hunger for money does not bring about equality, then what else will?

So again, the goals of the post-civil rights generation are power and influence, at whatever rung they can get it. "Are we here [at the best companies]? Yes, there are African Americans here," says Sean, still juggling expectant fatherhood and a product launch. "Are we in positions of influence and power and decision making? No, not really. So what does it matter."

We began this discussion with Richard's order to Black folks to leverage what we have. He's right. It is time. Why not? The mass is greater than all of its parts, no matter how isolated. Sean may be alone at BMS, and Alvin at Sony, and Kim at Dell, and the ambassador at Level 3 in Denver, and Oral at Marriott, but together they are more than just Onlys. Together, they are stronger, focused, and united. They are united by who they are: Black executives. That is a much stronger bond than any cause. Causes can fall out of favor, ideas can splinter, and beliefs can change. The fact that these are Black businessmen and businesswomen will remain.

This reminds me of something former Urban League president Hugh Price once said about this generation and survival. When the civil rights leader was head of the Urban League, he never got the attention he deserved. The mainstream media tends to be more in awe of Black leaders who are flamboyant—

with language or hairdos. In the 8 years that Price headed the League, he made it into the pages of the *New York Times* less than 100 times. Black Op-Ed columnist Bob Herbert was responsible for about half of those mentions. But if you wanted substance and vision, especially on economic empowerment issues, Price was the man. So his assessment of this generation is relevant. Trying to describe the post-civil rights generation, the polished, well-spoken activist stumbled just a bit. "I don't want to call them survivors," he finally concluded. "They are more than survivors. They are people who are extraordinarily talented and have learned the art of the deal. They've attended some of the nation's most prestigious schools, learned how to navigate the highest reaches of the systems, and they have *thrived.*"[7]

The key here is "thrived." It is a sign that the post-civil rights generation is already on its way to evoking Richard's words. Beyond Rage is all about surviving and thriving and using anything and everything you have to succeed, whatever your definition of success might be. This generation is thinking about success on their own terms, in their own minds, and under their own rules. That is the advantage of not being the Firsts.

Seeing things from this new perspective is kind of nice. Instead of being the end, breaking through ceilings has become the beginning. For this generation, the desire for more—a different more, that is—also means that they are in greater control of their own fate.

That's a spade in any game and a powerful card to have.

3

SISTAS UNITE! ARE BLACK WOMEN CORPORATE AMERICA'S FORGOTTEN THREAT?

Whatever's on my mind usually comes out of my mouth. You have to be true to who you are and be who you are. I am a Black woman. I never can leave that at the door.

—Susan Chapman, senior director, Level 3 Communications

*I*t was women's history month (March if you're wondering), and Dell Computers was in full celebration. The activities culminated in a panel discussion moderated by Michael Dell to showcase some of the company's top female executives. A hand shot up from the audience, and the question was simple. What did the women on the panel want to be doing in 5 years? For the most part, the responses from the row of corporate women were unmemorable—a lot of division goals or promotions-at-Dell answers. They *were* still sharing a stage with the company founder, after all. But, one response stood out.

"In 5 years I want to be leading my own business in the inner city," she said before her peers, her staff, and the company CEO. "My hope is to bring job creation and wealth to the African American community."

She was Kim Goodman, a 37-year-old VP with only 3 years at Dell. Months later, she still did not understand why people were so stunned by her honesty. "It is what is in my heart." That honesty was the inspiration for this book. Over and over again when I was talking to young Black executives, it was the women who tended to be bolder and clearer with their ideas about race. Although the men might share and support those sentiments, often it was women who were not afraid to make race the issue. Dripping with nothing-to-lose attitudes, they often sounded like Kim.

"My goal has always been the same," Kim explained one day. "I went into business so I could bring power to the African American community. I don't keep that a secret. I tell it to everyone. The only way African Americans are going to be uplifted is if we have major strides in the business front. The keys to improving the [Black] community are improvement in education and improvement in our participation in capitalism."

Black women are still at the bottom of the corporate ladder. Of the 5.3 million female managers at U.S. companies, only 974,000 are Black.[1] Black women earn approximately 64 cents for every dollar earned by white men—that's less than white women (74 cents), and less than Black men (78 cents).[2] But talk like Kim's makes them sound like the next power brokers of the race. In addition, the number of Black women in corporate ranks is increasing faster than the number of Black men, suggesting that we should be keeping an eye on those female executives instead.

When I first met Kim, she was a little younger, still single, using her maiden name, and somewhat new to the computer business. With a BA and MS from Stanford (the master's is in industrial engineering) and a MBA from Harvard, she has the kind of credentials that make employers' jaws drop. She spent 11 years in the consulting business, becoming the first Black female partner at Bain & Company in 1998. At Dell, she reports directly to Michael Dell and convinced him the switches that connect computer networks could be the PC maker's next golden egg. She is now leading the company's new aggressive push into the $17 billion switch market. Dell offered Kim a chance to head one of its big moneymaking divisions (the type of opportunity that executives traditionally pine for), but she opted to lead the company into uncharted territory instead. She sees starting the new venture for Dell as a test run for the business she hopes to start one day.

"I've learned a lot," she says almost more to herself than to me. "I've learned so much about my own strength and capability and power. What Kim Goodman brings. How much force I can bring to something when I choose to do something. I've learned a lot."

I was learning a lot from these women, too.

The first moment I talked to Susan "The Ambassador" Chapman, we just clicked. I had heard there was this no-nonsense, savvy corporate real estate executive out in ski country who knew how to shake things up. I had gotten her name third- and fourth-hand, so I wasn't sure if she would live up to the hype. Susan, 34, spends much of her time going back and forth to Europe brokering deals for Level 3 Communications, the Colorado-based technology company.

Because Susan has such a hectic travel schedule, catching up with her took some persistence. Our initial introduction was over the phone. After hello, it was obvious she had no clue who I was or why I would be calling. Apparently, none of those three or four hands ever mentioned that they'd given me her phone number. I offered to call her in the evening when she was out of the office and could talk frankly about what it was like to be a young Black woman in corporate America. Not necessary! she shot back so forcefully I almost felt silly for asking. "Anything I have to say I can say here. I have nothing to hide. They've all heard it before." Okay, I thought, the hype is warranted. I did quietly close my office door, though.

That is how the relationship started. Months later, during one of her trips to New York, we were laughing like old friends over fried chicken and cranberry juice. "There won't be any more opportunities around for the next generation if we don't fight," she says. Susan has a reputation at Level 3 for cutting through the bull. She has ripped senior leadership to shreds during meetings if she thinks their argument doesn't hold up. Often the only Black executive and the only woman in the room, she has been known to end meetings abruptly after only 10 minutes if a presentation looks to be a waste of time. One day, her boss confided to her that some of the managers complain about being afraid to work with her because she doesn't hold back, but tells just how it is, always. So her to-the-point assessment of the big issue facing Black professionals didn't surprise me. "It is up to us to keep the doors open," she says. "The worst thing we can do is get comfortable."

With a background in engineering and finance including an MBA and a master's in regional planning, Susan is a standout in the very middle-age, white male world of corporate real estate finance. Level 3 sells broadband infrastructure—it runs the fiber-optic network used by Internet service providers such as AOL, Microsoft, and Yahoo! In plain English, they provide the necessary circuit that allows the Internet to run. Susan is in the global real estate group. Real estate is a big deal for a company that needs to lay a lot of wire, even if it is fiber-optic. The group manages a portfolio of over 13 million square feet, which also houses technical facilities that enable the network to run, and is responsible for some $425 million in transactions in a typical year. When I caught up with Susan, she was also studying Mandarin Chinese in her spare time just to help keep her mind "juiced." Hanging on her wall at home back in Denver she has *Fortune* magazine's list of the 50 Most Powerful Black Executives, which includes top corporate standouts like Time Warner CEO Dick Parsons, Amex CEO Ken Chenault, Merrill Lynch CEO Stan O'Neal, Fannie Mae CEO Franklin Raines, and corporate board mogul Vernon Jordan. She has pasted her own picture in the middle of the spread. "This is what I'm aiming for."

These women generally don't back down from who they are and have reputations for speaking their minds. It almost becomes a necessity for survival. The profound assertiveness, strength, and militancy that these women show partly comes from the isolation they encounter. Kim occupies a unique space, like many senior level Black women in corporate America. Of the 100 or so people she interacts with at Dell regularly to do her job, from directors on up to senior VPs, there is only one other African American, a man, and one other woman, who is white. "To be an African American woman in corporate America . . . ," Kim just trails off, unable to finish her thought. "It's just . . . it's just . . ." She pauses, takes a deep breath, and begins again. "Let me be honest." Please do. "I think about my career in two phases—the building phase and the executive phase. In the building phase it was hard but manageable. In the VP phase it feels," she says, "harder."

As an executive, Kim has found relationship building much more important and says it can be difficult because people tend to be more comfortable with others like themselves. But when Black women reach the higher ranks, there is no one like them. "Not everyone is as accepting of an African American woman when you walk through the door. There is a difference when as a Black woman you are the leader and not just a helpful follower. There's more tension, there just is." High-ranking Black women all face the same thing.

IBM was recently named one of the three top companies for women of color. Among the computer company's accomplishments was the number of female executives of color, which had grown from 17 in 1995 to 74 in 2002. That includes all women of color—Hispanic, Asian, Native American, and Black.[3] IBM is one of the biggest companies in the nation (always in the Top 10 in the Fortune 500) with hundreds of thousands of employees, but in 2003 it needed fewer than 74 female Black executives (or less than 3 percent of all executives) to be applauded as a standout in corporate America. If Black executives in general exist as scattered islands across the corporate landscape, then Black women of significance in the business world are the island's secret beaches that searchers may stumble on once in a while. Such unspoiled essence may be hard to find, but totally refreshing and worth the trip.

Of any of the executives I talked to, Susan, the ambassador, was perhaps, the most isolated. Not only were there no Black executives at her level at her company, or pretty much in her industry, but she was also single and lived in an area of the country that offered little support for Black professionals.

Two weeks after Susan picked up and moved to the Rocky Mountain State by herself, a couple of self-proclaimed white supremacists shot a West African immigrant to death as he waited at a bus stop. This was Susan's introduction to Denver. Oumar Dia, 38, a hotel bellhop who sent $200 home to Senegal each week to support a wife and three kids, had left work shortly before midnight that night in November 1997. "You are a Nigger! Are you ready to die like a Nigger?" one of the skinheads shouted as he pulled the trigger. A single mother of two who came to Dia's aid was also shot in the back and was left paralyzed and bedridden for the rest of her life.[4]

Susan was more stunned by the lack of reaction in her new city than by the bus stop murder itself. Dia's murder was the culmination of 10 days of racist violence across Denver that also included a shoot-out that left a cop dead. "If this had been anywhere else [Jesse] Jackson would have been on the news, someone would have been protesting, churches would be hosting vigils. We didn't even have a single candle lit," said the Cleveland native, still in disbelief. In all fairness, there were a few demonstrations around the city. But the first rally with any significant turnout didn't happen for 2 weeks after the bus stop shooting. According to newspaper accounts, it drew a crowd of about 1,500 people, in a city with a population of approximately 500,000. So Susan's isolation is understandable.

It is what Black women like Susan turn that isolation into that makes them a serious force waiting to be recognized. Refusing to ignore race emboldens them. Susan, who sports a slightly lightened, close-cut natural, doesn't even feel the need to close her office door, remember. Speaking up can be freeing and empowering in itself.

In their book *Our Separate Ways: Black and White Women and the Struggle for Professional Identity,*[5] Professors Ella Bell and Stella Nkomo touch on the profound sense of isolation that Black women experience in corporate America. The authors conducted an 8-year study of more than 800 Black and white corporate women and concluded that Black women didn't feel that they had to submerge their true selves to get ahead. In contrast to their white counterparts, Black women learned how to be savvy about maintaining and asserting themselves in the organization. Essentially they say: "You know, I'm a Black woman. I want to maintain who I am. I will learn how to play this game in a different way." When I talked to Professor Bell soon after her book was published, I told her about the Kims and Susans out there. She wasn't surprised. She agreed this attitude was even more pronounced for young Black women whose tolerance of a power structure that white men still dominate is generally lower than that of their older counterparts. The younger women had expected to be embraced by a world that should have moved on by now. "When the reality hits these young women, it can be stunning," says Bell. "The armor that they put on can be almost impenetrable."

According to Bell, white men don't appreciate white women per se, but they know them—they are their wives, sisters, and daughters. They don't know Black men, but they are joined by gender and often use sports talk to bridge the gap.

But with Black women, there really isn't any connection. As a result, Bell argues, Black women become fiercely independent. Problems arise when they refuse to ask for help even when they need it. Their isolation leads to stereotypes that they are not team players, have massive chips on their shoulders, never smile, or don't hang out. It all adds up to the perfect recipe to kill a corporate career.

Separate Ways concludes that because Black women are faced with racism and sexism, they tend to be much more collective in their approach. When Black women go into a company, they seek each other out, network, have lunch, pass on information, and find ways of connecting among themselves to overcome their isolation at work.

This is significant because, in contrast to the groundbreaking generation, women are more likely to dominate the next generation and those thereafter. The Black gender gap has been talked about, discussed, studied, analyzed, and cried about to death. This is not the venue for adding to the rhetoric. For an update, pick up an issue of any Black women's magazine and there will surely be some mention of a successful Black woman who can't find an equally successful Black man. I talked to a young corporate woman whose mother told her on the day she graduated from college that her chances of finding a [Black] husband had just dropped. She hadn't even removed her cap and gown yet. The statistic that helped fuel a lot of this fear a few years ago—the one that stated there were more Black men in jail than in college—actually proved to be based on a major misunderstanding. Overall the number is true—in 2000 there were 791,600 Black men in jail and 603,000 Black men in college, just as the Justice Policy Institute published.[6] That is depressing and inexcusable, yes. But if the comparison includes only college-age Black men (ages 18 to 24), there were actually more in school than the 114,000 who were locked up.[7] Phew. Still, the numbers are nothing to celebrate.

In 1970, the numbers of Black men and women in college were nearly the same. Only 6 percent more Black women than Black men were enrolled. But after the women's lib movement, women of all colors started flocking into colleges and the professional ranks. Today, 56 percent of the overall college population is female. For African Americans, the numbers are even more striking: About 10 percent more Black females than males go to college, and females account for 67 percent of Black college graduates. Black women earn 69 percent of the Black master's degrees, 66 percent of the Black PhDs, and 58 percent of the Black professional degrees.[8]

In the end, 24 percent of all Black women will become part of the professional-managerial class compared with just 17 percent of Black men.[9] It is hard to ignore that, for whatever reasons (and that would fill a whole book in itself), Black men and women are ending up on different paths in life.

The examples are everywhere. In every newsroom I've ever worked in, there have always been more Black women than Black men. It is so common I usually don't even notice. It's hard not to notice, though, that those few Black men always hold higher positions in the newsroom than the mass of Black women.

In corporate circles, it's not really any different. Look around your office. "Next Generation" is a highly selective group of young Black professionals affiliated with the Executive Leadership Council. Started in 1986, ELC is a networking organization for senior Black executives of Fortune 500 companies who are no more than three steps away from the company's CEO. They consider themselves the most elite, which attracts some and repels others. Yet, their ranks have grown from 19 to 286 and include some definite movers and shakers across corporate America from Stan O'Neal to Ken Chenault. Next Generation is ELC's attempt to build a bridge to younger executives. These execs, in their 20s and 30s—all post-civil rights babies—haven't reached the top three levels of management at their companies, yet. ELC is confident that they will be there one day. The selection process for Next Generation is taxing, including a mandatory essay. The reward though is like getting a student pass to a show—all the benefits at half the price. What is noteworthy about ELC and its Next Generation spin-off is the shift. ELC is dominated by men, Next Generation members are mostly women. In between learning Mandarin and jet-setting to Europe, Susan was winding down her two-year term as president of Next Gen when our paths crossed. (Are you surprised?) She didn't think the difference in makeup between Next Gen and ELC was as significant as I did. To me, it signaled that women were poised to be the leaders of tomorrow. For Susan, it meant: "Sistas just have it together." Period. But having it together today directly affects what happens tomorrow.

The gender shift in Black professional ranks is important for Black folks in general. Typically in Black social commentary, women are not examined thoroughly. Unless the topic is tagged as a specific women's issue—from abortion, to dating, to domestic violence—the thoughts of Black women usually are not recorded. It is just assumed that Black is the same to all, men and women. What a misguided oversight! Black women and Black men will always be bonded by race and separated by gender. All Black folks do not think the same (really, we don't); likewise, Black women often see things differently from Black men on the same issues. I believe the ties of race are stronger than those of gender, the similarities outweigh the differences so Black women have more in common with Black men than they do with white women. Still, that does not mean that the gender differences in the thinking of Black people can be ignored.

If it is Black women who are getting ahead and if it is Black women who are making the concerted effort to unite, then it is likely that it will be Black women who have the potential organized clout to significantly uplift the race.

Traditionally, Black women have always served as a backbone, a moral anchor, and a driving force. But history has still tried its best to cast their contributions in a supporting role. Quick! Name a Black woman from the civil rights movement besides Rosa Parks. The fact that most people can't come up with a name has nothing to do with actual civil rights history but with how that history is told. Septima Clark, an educator from South Carolina, developed the Citizenship Schools across the South to teach Black adults to read and write so they could register to vote. Her work was crucial to the success of the movement and became a key part of the work of the Southern Christian Leadership Conference (SCLC), which laid the foundation for the civil rights movement. Ella Baker helped found the SCLC and the Student Nonviolent Coordinating Committee (SNCC), the other organization that served as the basis of the movement. Her fingerprint is all over the era, including her role as a key organizer of the Montgomery bus boycott. She also served as an advisor to Martin Luther King *and* Stokely Carmichael. Of Baker, King reportedly once said: "If Ella had been born a man, God only knows what she would have been able to do." Also often overlooked is Dorothy Height, who was the lone woman in the group of civil rights leaders known as the "Big Six" The other five members of the group were King, A. Phillip Randolph, Whitney Young, James Farmer, and Roy Wilkins; together, the six activists hammered out the plans for the movement. And Fannie Lou Hamer was the voice of the Mississippi Freedom Democratic Party, which declared a highly publicized war against the segregationist Mississippi delegation on the floor of the 1964 Democratic National Convention. The Freedom Party's protest became a pivotal moment that changed the nature of national party conventions thereafter. While in jail in Winona,

Mississippi, for leading a voter registration drive, Hamer was so viciously beaten that she suffered from the effects of her injuries for the rest of her life. On leaving jail, Hamer uttered the famous words, "I am sick and tired of being sick and tired." Even Rosa Parks was not just any tired bus rider. Parks was an elected officer of the Montgomery Chapter of the NAACP (as the chapter's first female member, she served as its secretary) who was very familiar with the nonviolent protest tools of the day. Her actions were *not* happenstance.

Black women have always significantly helped to uplift the race. The difference now is that they are rising to positions that traditionally bestow influence. Black women are also beginning to generate wealth. That gives them the clout to dictate discussion and influence the direction of Black folks. Well, ideally, they *should* be the guiding influences. At the very least, it will be harder to ignore the thought process of Black women. The feminization of Black power will gradually follow.

This shift is what I thought about when I heard a Black woman was running for president. Amid the endless onslaught of Democrats who announced their candidacy for the 2004 presidential race to unseat George W. Bush, somehow the stars aligned (or collided) and there were *two* Black candidates: The Rev. Al Sharpton, the New York based activist, and Carol Moseley Braun, the only Black woman ever to be elected to the U.S. Senate. Interesting. But Braun was probably running more against Sharpton than against Bush. Despite the legions of people who claim to be color-blind, the fact of the matter is, Black candidates do not win elected office without a solid majority of Black votes. These candidates can't win solely with Black votes, but they can't win without them either. Exit polls show that Black candidates elected to state office (Virginia Governor Wilder, Braun, Rep. J. C. Watts) averaged about 40 percent of the white vote while winning virtually all of the Black vote. So as much as Braun and Sharpton may like to argue that they are seeking broad appeal and are candidates for the masses, they need every Black vote possible to have any chance of winning. So Braun was running against Sharpton.

The internal fighting among Black folks is old news. Braun's unexpected entry into the race was encouraged by Democratic leadership and widely seen as a way to diminish Sharpton's chances. Sharpton makes the establishment nervous—Black and white. In case you missed it, he rose to national prominence in 1987 standing by the side of Tawana Brawley, a Black teenager from upstate New York. She had been found lying in a garbage bag smeared with feces and told a story about having been raped by a gang of white men, including an assistant district attorney from Dutchess County, New York. The story was later tagged a hoax. Since then, Sharpton has cleaned up his image by toning down his style a bit. He has gained praise for his relentless advocacy for Black people and the downtrodden in high-profile police brutality cases and served 90 days in jail to protest the Navy's bombing range in Vieques, Puerto Rico. He has also run for office several times in New York and always has finished better than the pundits predicted. In his 1994 Senate race, he grabbed 25 percent of the vote in the Democratic primary, including 80 percent of the Black vote. His appeal to Black voters crosses all class lines and has made him a force to be reckoned with for anyone wanting to be elected in the state.

So instead of conceding the Black vote to a candidate that the Democratic Party could not control, the best option was to split and weaken it. In walks Braun. (The plan assumes that Black voters will automatically pull the lever for a Black candidate and that a Black candidate would not attract a base beyond Black voters. This interpretation, which is based on stereotypes, is intrinsically condescending and offensive, even if often true.)

But Braun's entry is interesting because it is *possible*. It epitomizes the handoff among African Americans from men to women. It is why her candidacy is relevant to the next generation of Black executives. After serving just one term in the Senate (D-Ill), Braun lost her bid for reelection amid IRS questions on campaign finance. She was then exiled, er, appointed, ambassador to New Zealand by President Bill Clinton. Braun, an attorney who has held local, state, and national office, stands a mile away from Sharpton. She is not a minister, does not give fiery speeches—although she is good at generating a catchy sound bite—but brings a résumé loaded with all the appropriate posts and positions and everything you are supposed to do. With Braun, we have come to the point where a Black woman has enough clout, power, gumption, and legitimacy (because that is really the heart of her appeal), to challenge an established Black leader.

That shift will only continue and grow as the Black faces at the top—in business, politics, and the professions—are increasingly female.

This is why Black women cannot be ignored or pigeonholed, or relegated to a feminized ghetto of interests. At one point in the 2004 presidential race, there were two Black candidates. And on paper, not to knock Rev. Al one bit, the candidate with better *credentials* was the woman. This phenomenon—women—is the Black future.

For corporate America and the business world, that shift will also have a tremendous impact. As with any shift, there are significant differences between a mass of Black men and a mass of Black women. The most obvious is that despite the mass of Black women filling the corporate ranks, Black men have climbed higher. If we were to draw a pyramid of corporate power, from the top down it would be white men, huge gap, Black men, white women, and at the bottom, Black women. Some might argue that second place is a toss-up between Black men and white women. In the past few years, a significant number of white women have managed to climb through the cracks in the glass ceiling. Carly Fiorina is CEO of Hewlett-Packard, Meg Whitman is CEO of eBay, Ann Mulcahny is CEO of Xerox, and Pat Russo is CEO of Lucent. Although Andrea Jung, CEO of Avon, is not white, she's also not Black—for this discussion that is what matters. And these are just the company CEOs; go a step down to divisions or business units (Ann More is CEO of Time Inc. and Betsy Holden is co-CEO of Kraft), and the group swells further. If you look at the numbers alone, white women (and Andrea) have outstripped Black men. But look at the power and influence that come with the posts of those few Black men at the top. Dick Parsons is CEO of Time Warner, the most powerful media company in the world; Stan O'Neal is CEO of Merrill Lynch, the nation's largest brokerage house; Ken Chenault is CEO of American Express, the mega credit card and financial services company; and Franklin Raines is CEO of Fannie Mae, the largest mortgage financing firm in the United States as well as one of the most widely held stocks. These Black men control some of the most powerful companies in the nation. The power that comes with that is unquestioned. The likes of Xerox, Kraft, Avon, and eBay can't really compare. So in my pyramid, Black men go above white women.

Regardless of any such disputes, at the bottom of every pyramid are Black women. Ann Fudge, CEO of ad firm Young & Rubicam, is the highest-ranking Black woman in corporate America—hands down. After a career in packaged goods, including key posts at Kraft, General Foods, and General Mills, she became the first Black executive to lead a major advertising agency. But she is not near the level of Dick Parsons et al. Young & Rubicam, a major firm in its industry, is still just one of the subsidiaries of London-based WPP Group, the world's biggest advertising company. And she's the top Black woman.

The more significant difference that the shift brings is the view. When you are at the bottom of the ladder, as Black women are, you have nothing to lose. And that can be a powerful motivator.

In fact, Black women "are the least satisfied [of all groups of women] and overall least likely to stay in their current jobs," says Sheila Wellington, president of Catalyst, a research organization that studies corporate women. If this generation, in general, is turning its rage into action (which it is), then Black women, as the most dissatisfied sector, should be a hotbed for that kind of rage-fueled action (they are). That Black women are frustrated, or have rage, is not new. What is new is the clout that these women now have, which enables them to direct their rage and, in turn, achieve even more clout.

There are some things you just have to come right out and say: The most common reason Black women become entrepreneurs is discrimination. According to the Center for Women's Business Research, 36 percent of Black women said they became entrepreneurs after hitting the glass ceiling. Only 12 percent of Hispanic women and 21 percent of white women surveyed said that hitting a glass ceiling pushed them into entrepreneurship. What does it mean? It means that Black women—the corporate types dealing with the glass ceiling—are turning to action. Discrimination may be why they want to start their own business, but the goals of these businesswomen are also very different from the goals of others. Black women, more than any other female business owners, start businesses for altruistic reasons. By owning their own business, 92 percent of Black women are hoping that they can serve as role models and 83 percent want to make a difference in their communities through business ownership.[10]

This is what happens when rage turns into action. These educated, highly trained women don't put up with much. That is why they are dissatisfied with their status on the pyramid. The Blackprint, doing this now to do that later, is what guides them. Which means that Black women may just be corporate America's overlooked threat.

Are we ready for a movement led by women? I hope so. But you never know. When I was a sophomore in college, I took a history seminar on Black nationalism. It was the early 1990s, and we were a tight-knit group of mostly Black students majoring in history. Our professor was one of the highest ranking Black professors at the school at that time. He usually devoted his time to research and seldom mingled with undergraduates. At the end of the semester, we each had to conduct one of the weekly sessions, develop a lesson, assign reading, and lead a discussion. After a semester of hearing about Marcus Garvey, Malcolm X, Bobby Seale, and Huey Newton, I decided to focus my discussion on the writings of bell hooks when it came time for my week. At 19, I naively thought I had discovered something. I proudly schooled the group on the author's fiery words on the intersection of racism, sexism, and classism, and how no discussion that includes one without the others was worth having. Here, in hooks, was a Black woman who refused to let anyone forget that. She was neither just Black nor just a woman and that was the point. Instead, she wanted the world to see things from her whole point of view, as a Black woman. Up until that point, feminism, for me, was something that sounded good in theory but was missing for a woman of color. Likewise, Black nationalism lectures and the Black power discussions that sprang forth were some of the most meaningful I would hear in college, but as a woman, I thought that they also were missing something. Then I found the section of the library that housed the words of hooks, Michele Wallace, Audre Lorde, and a whole school of people who combined gender and race. So I used my lecture to argue that Black feminism was the most militant brand of Black power. In the simple, naive logic of a 19-year-old, if Black women were at the bottom rung of Black society, then to uplift the race, you should focus on lifting the bottom rung–women. Well, maybe it wasn't so naive.

My professor, a proud member of the civil rights generation, did not approve. In fact, he was angry. Until that day, I hadn't been yelled at in class since elementary school. My argument was disrespectful to Black nationalist thought and Black power theories, he said. My choice was a deviation from the subject matter, irrelevant, and showed no understanding of the history he had just spent a semester trying to teach me, he said. And I would not get credit for the assignment. Not the reaction I was expecting. At the time, the only thing he said that mattered to my college brain was the last part, no credit. The rest I didn't really pay attention to. He was just a sexist jackass, I thought.

Since then though, the rest of what he said continues to play back in my mind. I still think he's a sexist jackass. But, lately, I've come to think the rest of what he said was more a reflection of a failure to recognize that shift than of his own insecurities and obvious character flaws. He couldn't see what or how women mattered to a Black movement. Sitting in a classroom at an Ivy League school where most of my Black classmates were women, I couldn't see how women could *not* matter. That's why we were there, to matter, and for most of us, to matter for African Americans.

It never occurred to me that focusing a Black power discussion around women was a big deal, partly because that is what my generation is all about. There is no difference; there is no separation. When Black professional women speak out, there is no line between various rhetoric and movements. It is all one, with one goal. That is why Kim at Dell can talk freely and openly about how she is going to uplift the race on the back of what she learns in the corporate world. Not that her male counterparts necessarily disagree. There isn't much difference between her talk and that of say, Richard Gay at Booz

Allen. Both are determined not to compromise themselves, their Blackness shall we say, to succeed in the system. They both are using that system—the business world—to uplift Black people. But the Kims seem a bit more forceful than the Richards, although maybe it's my own bias that sees it that way. Either way, we are going to get to a point soon where there will be many more Kims than Richards in those well-positioned spots that matter. And that's a big difference.

Two shifts are happening here. First, this generation is turning to economics and business as the answer. That is the Beyond Rage factor. Once we reach that point, the demographic shift of the Black corporate world from men to women will occur. The "movement," using its broadest, most lenient definition—the uplifting of Black people—will be at a crossroads. That means the next leaders will likely be Black businesswomen. I don't believe this is going to happen tomorrow—remember, there are only four Black CEOs of Fortune 500 companies right now, and none are women. But logically, that is the direction the movement is moving toward.

This has been, by far, the hardest chapter for me to write. This is my experience. Talking to Kim, to Susan, and to the many other women who are not named, I felt that the words could be mine. When Professor Bell spoke of the Black female chip on the shoulder, I've bent under that weight. Or when Kim admitted how alone it all feels sometimes, I knew exactly, in the pit of my gut, what she was saying. At my last meeting with Susan, the ambassador, we reached out to hug. It was supposed to be goodbye, but it sure felt more like support, an I-feel-your-pain embrace. I know the isolation, the thought process, the expectations, the commitment, the dreams and desires of these women because I am a Black woman trying to make a difference in a white world, too. And it is hard.

Some people are comforted when they find out they are not the only ones who have these feelings. It helps to discover they are not the only ones isolated, frustrated, and angry. It is affirming to know that others know exactly what you are going through and are also going through it. Susan exhaled when I also couldn't quite grasp how a room full of her coworkers could be stumped over her Jeopardy question about the double meaning behind their CEO's name, Jim Crow(e). There's a comfort when you find out that you aren't crazy. The problem is, I never really thought I was crazy. Not getting the Jim Crow(e) connection is what is crazy to me. So when I realized that it was *not* just me, it was overwhelming. How could what I'd been going through—the isolation, the frustration, the weight—*not* just be here, but everywhere? How?

It could be depressing to dwell on that. For a good long—okay, longer than that—moment it was. But then, I exhaled as the thought hit me: If Black women are the next power brokers of the race, then it won't be that bad. As someone once said: We do have it together.

4

DISSED BY DIVERSITY: HOW DIVERSITY BECAME A DIRTY WORD

Race was the sacrificial lamb to launch diversity and make it palatable to corporate America.

— Lisa Willis Johnson, the Society for Human Resource Management's diversity chair.

I fought like hell to get that quote into the conservative pages of *Fortune* magazine, the newsstand's most faithful chronicle of corporate America. It was almost 2 years ago during the preparation of the magazine's annual diversity issue— a showcase for its ranking of the 50 "Best Companies for Minorities." The generally positive package didn't have much room for my story about the hoax of corporate diversity programs. As a result, my story kept getting shorter and shorter and the quote kept getting the ax.

One day when I was talking to Oral Muir, the nugget-wielding Marriott e-commerce executive, he blurted out in a fit of frustration: "Nothing drives me more crazy than the whole color-blind thing. It drives me nuts!" I immediately flashed back to Lisa and her criticism of corporate diversity programs. After more than a decade in human resources, Lisa's biggest complaint about these programs was that, despite their perception, they really don't focus much attention on race. Oral's and Lisa's comments are the flip sides of the same coin. Both are taking issue because race has been removed from the equation. Their criticisms come from the same place. They say the same thing: Race is important; therefore, it deserves center stage. It is not something that should be ignored. It is not something that can be ignored. Therefore, those who agree with Lisa are probably also going nuts like Oral.

To address the issue of diversity without giving racial differences center stage is to ignore one of our most defining characteristics.

To look at Oral and claim not to see he is a Black man is naive. That may not be *all* you see, but you see it. To be color-blind means that you just never see it. Is any one of us that unobservant?

The interesting thing about diversity and color blindness is that both are supposed to be good for us. Recognizing or re-specting our differences and ignoring our differences are both somehow a good thing. Lisa and Oral express frustration be-cause, despite the best of intentions, something is not working.

Today, more than 75 percent of Fortune 500 companies boast some sort of diversity initiative. At some companies, the Chief Diversity Officer (CDO) occupies the executive suite along with the CEO, CFO, and other senior officers. When the University of Michigan's use of race in admissions came under fire in 2003, putting the future of affirmative action in jeopardy, corporate America stuck its neck out in support of the university. Sixty-eight of the biggest Fortune 500 companies, including IBM, General Electric, Nike, and GM, submitted a record number of briefs to the Supreme Court in support of affirmative action. The reason? Because these companies say they want to preserve *diversity* in the corporate ranks. Under the corporate logic, affirmative action guaran-tees that graduating classes—the recruitment pool for Ameri-can companies—will be diverse, thus making it easier for companies to build diverse workforces. The U.S. Supreme Court agrees. In the *Michigan* case, affirmative action was upheld by a one-vote margin for one reason: diversity. In her majority opinion, Justice Sandra Day O'Connor used Justice Lewis Powell's opinion in the 1978 *Bakke* case as a springboard. Powell argued that race could be used as a "plus factor" in admission and that diversity is a "compelling state interest."[1] At the time, the concept of diversity as a supporting factor for affirmative action was considered tangential to the argument. Powell's argument was issued as a solitary opinion.[2] But 25 years later when the *Michigan* decision came down from the court, the issue was 100 percent about diversity. Powell's diversity argument moved from single opinion to the majority. O'Connor also gave Powell's argument teeth by using corporate America's support for diversity as proof that it is necessary.[3]

In an instant, the goal of affirmative action officially morphed from remedying past discrimination to preserving future diversity. The Bush administration even used diversity to praise the decision that it had fought to prevent. In his official statement after the ruling, President Bush said: "I applaud the Supreme Court for recognizing the value of diversity on our nation's campuses. Diversity is one of America's greatest strengths. Today's decision seeks a careful balance between the goal of campus diversity and the fundamental principle of equal treatment under the law." Never mind that the Bush administration previously argued that Michigan's affirmative action program was unconstitutional. Of Bush's bizarre concession speech, the *New York Times* concluded: "Today's rulings may also demonstrate that it is now a rare officeholder who will not show some deference to the concept of diversity."[4]

The same could be said for the business world. It is probably safe to assume that there is not a CEO of any major company who doesn't have something good to say, publicly, about diversity at this point. "The belief in diversity is not something that is argued anymore in business. It is a factor of being in business," said James Hackett, CEO of Steelcase, the office furniture company, after the Supreme Court decision. Hackett is credited with spearheading the corporate campaign, including the Friend of the court briefs, to support the University of Michigan affirmative action programs.[5]

Sure, there are slipups of the Trent Lott variety now and then. (One can only guess what is being uttered in the privacy of executive bathroom suites.) But, can you imagine a modern-day CEO willing to officially wash his hands in public of what has become such a lofty goal as diversity? A CEO who would come out and say: Honestly, we have enough minorities! I only trust a team that looks just like me! Please, send your résumé somewhere else! It's just not going to happen; people are smarter than that now. We live in a post-PC world where indirectness rules and language is always coded. "Today Jim Crow Jr. is an Ivy Leaguer who's smarter and slicker than his grandfather was," blasted Leroy Warren, chairman of the NAACP Federal Task Force on Discrimination in the Workplace, from the pages of the *Wall Street Journal* in the Spring of 2000. "But the end result is the same."[6] Indeed, if a bad gift is wrapped in a nice package it's still a bad gift.

The hoax of corporate diversity programs is that such programs help Black folks (or other racial minorities). In reality, they help *a lot* of people. That is fine and why they should stick around. But it isn't always good news for Black folks.

In an effort to avoid the antagonism created by affirmative action, diversity has become a catchall term that embraces everything. Whereas affirmative action originally was identified with African Americans, and sometimes Latinos, corporate diversity programs have come to include any type of "other" imaginable. As a result, diversity has come to mean virtually nothing. Diversity sacrificed its bite to become acceptable.

That broader definition usually includes women, the disabled, homosexuals, and religious minorities. In some industries, seniors are on the list. I've even seen single mothers, atheists, communication style (low talkers versus screamers?–I don't know), career experience, hometowns, and just about anything else that technically may be underrepresented in a specific corporate setting. They *all* fall under diversity programs. And that is the problem.

Dizzied by the choices, one Fortune 500 HR executive complained to me that her company officially defines diversity as: "Everyone with a different perspective or idea." In fact, that's not too far from the official definition of diversity set by the Society for Human Resource Management (the HR trade group and thus the barometer of HR policy). SHRM dictates that diversity includes "an infinite range of individuals' unique characteristics and experiences."

Then add to that long list, African Americans, Latinos, Asians, and Native Americans.

In 1995, the diversity initiative at one major retail company covered two groups: women and minorities. Six years later, it had swelled to include 26 different groups of people meaning that race is a very small kernel of today's diversity initiatives. Not that targeting all these groups is necessarily bad, or that corporate America shouldn't be interested in creating a welcoming environment to a diverse group of thoughts, views, experiences, and, yes, people. Do you remember the McPizza, though? McDonald's has already found out how hard it is to do everything.

For the post-civil rights generation, focused on race, corporate America's one-love approach smacks of naïveté, denial, and insensitivity. They like things direct and honest, no matter how bad the news. Anything less than that and intentions become suspect. Empowered by their credentials, they do not feel the need to be accommodating to move ahead. But given those credentials, race becomes the only logical explanation when they don't move ahead. Trying to make sense of the frustration they feel, this generation is more likely to view things through a colorized lens, which they have concluded will never be wiped clean. "Being a Black man in corporate America is no different than anywhere else. It is very difficult," says Alvin, at Sony with the bull___ title. "Race does matter. Recognize that it matters. But there is only so much you can do about it, though. What do I do? I still expect to win."

Some may argue that the lens limits this generation. I think it makes it stronger. Keeping race in mind helps this generation stay focused. They don't have to add race to the equation later, because it is already sitting front and center. More importantly, they are not trying to change the view but trying to succeed despite the lens. That's why the notion of color blindness drives some people nuts. "I *am* different," declares Oral. "That doesn't mean treat me with less respect but it serves no purpose to think that we are all the same."

Surprisingly, some HR professionals are starting to sound a bit more like Oral. They include staffing experts who think diversity's de-emphasis on race is hurting the cause as well as HR executives who are troubled by the array of choices in the diversity programs they administer. *HR Focus,* the magazine that covers the entire industry, recently declared that soft-pedaling race was the top "worst practice" that corporate diversity programs can engage in. It concluded that making the definition of diversity too broad has hurt more than it has helped. The publication warned: "Replacing direct language with 'safe' words signals a lack of clarity or a lack of commitment to the world of diversity. Issues must be clearly defined and articulated before they can be changed."[7] Exactly.

Those who have the most to gain from fuzzy definitions are the diversity advocates themselves. Think about it. Diversity is a multibillion-dollar industry that includes pricey consultants, experts, products, seminars, and even games. Basically, there's no barrier to entry. It requires no degree, no certification process, and no common credential for people to claim to be diversity gurus. Virtually anyone can hang up a shingle and proclaim their expertise. In 2000, more than 5,000 diversity consultants were out there vying to tell corporate America whatever it needs to know about diversity.[8] Yes, some are true believers in diversity—the cause. But there's no denying that the diversity *industry* is good business. It is estimated that companies spend $8 billion a year on diversity initiatives.[9] Diversity is as much a business as software is for Microsoft and movies are for Hollywood. And race, because of its divisiveness and its emotional baggage, is bad for business. At one time, in a world before Texaco-size lawsuits, and people-of-color classifications, the diversity industry was dominated by minority-owned firms that were working just as hard to spread a message as they were to make a buck. These days, the message *is* the buck. The business opportunity is so tempting that mainstream firms have launched diversity practices and publications, or generally have found some way to get their hand in the industry. The biggest publications spreading the diversity message—DiversityInc., Cultural Diversity at Work, and Diversity Monitor—were all started by mainstream companies.

If you are selling diversity services, it only makes sense to broaden the definition of diversity to its outer limits. Broaden the product appeal and you increase the sale potential. If you include as many different types of people as possible under the umbrella of diversity, you are bound to hit one thing that a customer may be interested in. It is like a game of darts—if you make the target big enough, at least one dart is bound to find its mark.

That is why diversity is increasingly also a white thing. Under this broad definition, there are even diversity programs out there that devote their attention entirely to white men. Consultant firms with names like Inclusivity, EqualVoice, and Kaleidoscope stress recognizing the diversity of white men and their role in the diversity debate. The White Men's Caucus is a four-day diversity retreat just for white men. Held each spring, at a private mountaintop ranch about a two-hour drive from Portland, Oregon, the Caucus caters to approximately 20 executives at a time and has a waiting list months deep. Executives indulge in touchy-feely powwows, where their needs and contributions to diversity are the focus. Judging from program testimonials, some participants come away with a better understanding of their "own guilt" and "participation in corporate oppression" concerning minorities. More significantly, though, others learn to value their own individuality as white men and what contributions they bring to a diverse workforce.

This is the problem with this kind of approach: For diversity to succeed, it makes sense to focus at some level on white men since they hold the power now. Convince this group, the logic goes, and everything else will fall into place. But this approach also raises serious issues. The danger is that it misplaces the emphasis. It is a backdoor way of approaching a subject, which may make it easier to lose focus on the real issue. Should the needs of white men really be the focus of diversity efforts? There is something inherently wrong, almost backward, about subscribing to a diversity program that excludes more people than it includes. Don't you think?

Although the white-man approach still represents a minority of diversity teachings, it is gaining popularity. One book from this school that is making the rounds among corporate managers is *The Self-Interest in Diversity for Straight, White, American-Born Male Managers,* written by Seattle-based diversity consultant Chuck Shelton. Wal-Mart, the nation's largest company, was so impressed with Shelton's teachings about the potential diversity contributions of white men that he became one of the first and only outside diversity consultant the retailer has ever hired.

Regardless of the business case, diversity's McPizza approach makes little sense from a people relations standpoint. Whenever corporations try to do everything, someone is left unsatisfied. Mandatory diversity seminars or training programs can encounter just as much eye-rolling resistance from Black executives as from white. It is not that they do not support the goal. But the general consensus is that it is going to be a waste of time. Even if everyone herded into the room agrees the goal is something that they all should care about, the didactic tone usually accompanying that process makes the participants feel as if they are being forced to eat their vegetables. To gauge just how deep the dissatisfaction runs, I decided to ask the ambassador of Black America—Susan back at Level 3—what she thought of corporate diversity initiatives. From her Colorado office, she mouthed off for an impassioned 20 minutes about the importance and need for such programs. "But are they effective?" I asked. "No!" the ambassador answered. Then there was silence.

Part of the skepticism from this generation stems from their introduction to the diversity movement. This is a generation that came of age during the height of the battle over affirmative action. It is hard to remember now how vicious the fights were and how emotionally charged the discussion was over affirmative action. But, it gripped the nation just as this post-civil rights generation was putting the program to the test and heading off to the best colleges in the country.

Unlike previous generations, this generation—white and Black—was far enough removed from the nation's most painful racial memories that it was easy to feel disconnected. In-your-face discrimination was harder to find—people were not being arrested anymore for trying to buy lunch at Woolworth's. That doesn't mean *Jim Crow Jr.* doesn't exist—it is just easy for some to overlook. Because legal segregation was history before the post-civil rights babies were born, whites of this generation often feel no responsibility for crimes that they think were very much in the past. Instead, they feel they are being punished for wrongs that they had nothing to do with. The concept of white privilege—the inherent benefit that is gained when skin is white—is considered out of date. Instead, whites now feel wronged. Thus, affirmative action has drawn their resentment because it is a program meant to right past wrongs in hopes of leveling a playing field that was made deliberately uneven for years.

Like the death penalty or abortion, affirmative action was an emotional debate. Chances were that the angry voices on the other side of the issue were once friends, classmates, or peers—the ones who sported turtlenecks and bowl haircuts in the cafeterias of our memories. During the civil rights era, the enemy was clear. But this generation has found themselves fighting against people they had never thought could be enemies. It is a level of betrayal that leaves deep scars. Trust is the biggest casualty of such a battle. Trample on trust too much and it eventually gets destroyed—hence, this generation's skepticism and cynicism.

By the time these young people surfaced for the workforce in the early 1990s, affirmative action dropped from the public's lips less often because *diversity* had become the flavor du jour. It was almost 20 years ago, back in 1987, that the Hudson Institute released its *Workforce 2000* report that introduced diversity to American business. Commissioned by the Department of Labor, *Workforce 2000: Work and Workers for the 21st Century,* was a demographic outlook for the twenty-first century. It discussed such trends as the aging workforce, the phenomenon of temporary workers, and the widening skill gap between workers and jobs.

The *Workforce 2000* study also projected that white men in the work world were an endangered species. Using census data, birth rates, and demographic patterns, the researchers predicted that by the year 2000 white men would account for only 10 percent of the new entrants in the labor force. Instead, the pool of new workers would overwhelmingly comprise minorities and women.

These days, such a projection seems obvious. We have been hearing about the majority minority for years. By as early as 2005, minorities–African Americans, Hispanics, and Asians–will account for one third of the country's population. By 2060, the scales are expected to tip much further, and 51 percent of the nation's population will be people of color.[10] What does that mean? It means today, if you are over 70 years old there is a 20 percent chance you are a person of color. If you are under 40, your chances inch up to 50 percent. And if you are 10 or younger, at this very moment, there is a 75 percent chance that you are a person of color.[11] But, at the time the report was released, 47 percent of new workers were white men. So, the thought that white men wouldn't always be the army that kept American business running was, well, out there. By bucking such a common assumption, *Workforce 2000* eventually became one of the most influential studies on the American workplace. The revelation that the workforce of the future was shades of brown planted the seed for the corporate diversity movement. *Workforce 2000* became part of the corporate lingo, spawning books, WF2000 consultants, and organizations.

The lightbulb didn't go off immediately. In fact, *Workforce 2000* originally did not make much of an impact. In the summer of 1987, the media barely noticed the report's predictions about the growing impact of people of color on the labor force. Instead, the business press was busy with coverage of insider trading scandals, the widening trade deficit, and the stock market crash. With so much going on, there was neither time nor space to devote to a think tank's predictions about the next decade. For more than a year, none of the major news organizations paid any significant attention to the report's findings.

On the rare instance when *Workforce 2000* was mentioned in the press, it was usually in reference to the study's research about the plight of older workers, not on its projections about minorities. Gradually, this began to change, though. Who knows why—slow news days maybe—but the 10 percent statistic started to get noticed.

By 1990, the message was out. Suddenly, *Workforce 2000,* and the increased significance of the minority labor force, was everywhere. A survey that year found that 75 percent of Fortune 500 companies were now concerned with the issue. Of those, 30 percent were training managers to value diversity.[12] Corporate America was suddenly scared by the reality of a future workforce that they knew nothing about. No one wanted to be caught behind in the recruitment war. The mob was racing toward diversity, by any means necessary.

Thus, "diversity," with its image of inclusiveness and serving everyone, immediately had the support that affirmative action could have only dreamed about. Ironic, isn't it? It amazes me that people can be so in favor of one program that supposedly helps minorities (diversity), while being so vehemently against another program that also claims to help minorities (affirmative action). But then when it comes to race, the debate is not necessarily dripping with logic.

Whatever diversity *is* might be hard to pin down, but what it is *not* is pretty clear. It isn't a legal obligation to give minorities and women preference in hiring or promotion in the hopes of elevating their status to the levels of white men. That would be affirmative action. Diversity is not a government mandate. Diversity does not have the power of the federal government behind it as affirmative action does (or at least does for the moment). This major difference should never be overlooked. Although the overall intentions might be similar between diversity and affirmative action in terms of bringing aboard minorities, diversity will always be a poor substitute.

By definition, diversity will never have the power or clout behind it of a government-mandated program. You can't take your boss to court for not introducing a diversity seminar or sending your team on the latest diversity retreat.

There are also no benchmarks of success for a diversity initiative. Call me cynical (I am part of the post-civil rights generation, after all), but I'd bet that is also part of diversity's appeal. In the transformation from affirmative action to diversity, corporate America has created a situation where they can portray themselves as being concerned with minority issues without having to be held accountable. Public image is important; it affects business, and discrimination suits are not smart marketing. No one wants to be the next Coca-Cola or Texaco. So, the business world has nothing to lose by telling people what they want to hear.

It is always easier to give the *impression* that you are something else, instead of actually doing the work to change. (Isn't that Dating 101?) Diversity works well for corporate America by allowing it to portray the image of caring whether everyone is at the table and getting along even if no one has done a thing to make sure that there is truth behind the image.

As in any relationship, though, diversity's honeymoon didn't last too long. The economy hit a rough patch, and all of a sudden diversity didn't seem like such a good idea anymore. When you are out of work, out of money, and going through tough times, there is no room to be sympathetic to the plights of others. It isn't a coincidence that bias crimes go up when the economy goes bad.

The diversity backlash started to go public about 1993. A story in *Newsweek* that year reported that 56 percent of white men now believed that they were losing the advantage in terms of jobs.[13] By 1994 *BusinessWeek* splashed across its cover "White, Male, and Worried." The 3,000-word story detailed the resentment, frustrations, and fear that white men felt across corporate

America in the wake of the new interest in diversity. The story quoted one strategic consultant in Cambridge who concluded that "White male" was the nation's newest curse word. Referring to "White male," he said, "We all know that's not a compliment." Letters poured in from white men accusing diversity efforts of stealing their jobs. One out-of-work airport baggage carrier signed his angry rant about people of color and women, "Wrong pigment, Wrong plumbing."[14]

The post-civil rights generation was new to the workforce when this backlash was taking hold. So they entered offices sometimes laced with resentment. Making it worse, this generation had already been through this once before. Years earlier they had been hit with the fallout from affirmative action and were accused of stealing spots in universities; now they were accused of stealing jobs, this time in the name of diversity. It was the worst kind of déjà vu. This explains a little bit of the eye rolling back at the office when the diversity seminar herding begins.

The eye rolling is a sign of the skeptical distrust that flows through today's Black executives. This is a very show-me generation, which means it values actions, not words; memories of promises that have already been broken are common. Working While Black means that they have already been passed up climbing the ladder. Although this generation is moving higher, faster, there are still too many days when they are the only Black face in the room. It is proof for them that despite the official stand on diversity, something just isn't working.

Let me be clear: This is not a right-wing rant against diversity. I am not arguing that color blindness will save the day, either; nor am I suggesting that this generation thinks minority concerns should be ignored—quite the opposite. In fact, Black executives I interviewed who voiced concerns about diversity initiatives also went out of their way to argue that these programs should in no way be abandoned. They support

94

anything that could ultimately fill the ranks with more Black faces. But, they are weary of placing complete faith in such programs and are blaming the methods, not the goal. Despite the rhetoric, their everyday existence in the offices of our biggest and best companies makes them skeptical that these programs get the full support necessary for success. The unsatisfactory results of these diversity initiatives raise doubts about the company's commitment. Are these programs hollow? If diversity is so important, why are these initiatives so marginalized? (This last question was probably the most common critique made by this generation.) Because a major problem with diversity's credibility is its de-emphasis on race, young Black executives are left wondering what to believe.

To understand their muted endorsement, consider the reality of corporate diversity initiatives. Any HR executive, management consultant, and even the bulk of those self-proclaimed diversity experts will tell you the biggest determining factor in the success of a diversity effort is support from the top. Cultural change requires a top-down approach. Actions at the top directly affect behavior throughout an organization. Although 75 percent of Fortune 500 companies offer some type of diversity initiative, only 11 percent of those companies report that their CEOs initiated the program. In fact, about half of the 75 percent admit that their CEO played only a minimal role in the implementation of or participation in such programs.[15] So, again, how can we believe that these programs are a priority?

Even supporters would admit that most diversity activities have not been held to the same level of accountability as other human-resource initiatives; the criteria are certainly far less stringent than those used for profit-and-loss (P&L) decisions. "If they were evaluated vigorously the results would be disturbing," says Carol Kulik, management professor at Arizona State University. "How would you feel if you invested all this money and found out that it had no effect? I think that's true when you talk about changing day-to-day relations at work. Companies do it for other reasons: legal protection, symbolism."[16]

Where does that leave the business case for diversity? Under attack. The biggest selling point for diversity is that it is simply good business. "I've never used the expression 'It's the right thing to do,'" says Ivan Seidenberg, CEO of Verizon, which has a reputation for nurturing Black executives. "I think it's a '70s expression. Diversity is no more right than upgrading facilities. It is something you have to do for the business."

The argument that diversity is good for business makes sense, but there aren't any numbers to tell us *how* good. The numbers that are often thrown around concern things like buying power and market share. A diverse workforce is seen as a necessity to take full advantage of the growing global economy and the browning of America. Companies are betting that it will be easier to get access to these growing markets if their workforce reflects them. Black buying power is expected to increase 170 percent to $853 billion by 2007. Minority buying power—Black, Asian, and Native American—is expected to triple by 2007 totaling almost $1.4 trillion. (Since Latinos can be of any race, their buying was estimated separately and is expected to increase 315 percent by 2007 to $926 billion.)[17] Sure these figures are impressive. But impressive to whom? Knowing who will have the buying power makes it easy for, say, a Procter & Gamble to see that they need to understand people of color better if they want to sell them more tubes of Crest toothpaste. (As the master marketer of consumer products, Procter & Gamble is now increasing its advertising efforts to attract Black consumers. Not only are they increasing the stable of brands that will get Black marketing campaigns, they also are including Black ad agencies with mainstream marketing efforts in recognition that the influence of Black consumers is much larger than just Black folks.) But what about companies that are not pushing consumer goods?

There, buying power becomes meaningless. It may be harder to believe diversity will matter to the bottom line of companies that don't depend on average shoppers.

As long as diversity efforts are not held accountable, they will be vulnerable to criticism. Today, much of the diversity industry is focused on recruitment. If the percentage of white men is diminishing, recruitment efforts must broaden their net; otherwise companies risk passing up some of the best and brightest. That's admirable, but, for the bottom line, more important than hiring people from everywhere is actually keeping them. Replacing a lost employee generally costs four times that employee's salary when recruitment and training costs are factored in. Black turnover rates are 40 percent higher than the rate for their white counterparts. (Frustration over the lack of career opportunities is the key culprit.)[18] That is a lot of money. For diversity to be successful, it can no longer ignore such costs. If the business case is to be taken seriously, retention should be a much bigger part of the discussion than it is today. Recruitment means nothing without retention.

The movement's shaky foundation of support is partly why, in the spring of 2003, the sins of an incompetent newspaper reporter quickly came to symbolize all that is wrong with diversity. Jayson Blair was an unscrupulous reporter for the *New York Times*. He had this nasty habit of plagiarizing stories from other newspapers. When he couldn't find anything to steal, he made it up. Often assigned to do the features and sidebars related to major news events of the day, his juicy fictitious details would land his stories on the front page of the nation's most respected newspaper. He fabricated stories describing hospital bedside chats with battle-injured marines back from Iraq. In a profile of rescued army private Jessica Lynch, he touchingly described her father tearing up on his hilltop porch overlooking tobacco fields and cattle pastures. Lynch's family lives in a valley, not on a hill, among other houses with no tobacco or pastures in sight. During the Maryland sniper case that gripped the nation, Blair wrote confession details about anger and resentment that sniper suspect John Muhammad never uttered. For months, the national correspondent did not leave his apartment in Brooklyn to investigate a single story even though the datelines of his articles placed the young reporter zipping around the country from Hunt Valley, Maryland, to Cleveland, to Los Fresnos, Texas.[19] He deceived his editors and his readers.

Jayson Blair is Black.

That means that when his dishonesty was finally uncovered, the issue quickly stopped being about one crummy reporter but became an attack on diversity in the newsroom and beyond. Did Blair get his job over more qualified candidates because he was Black? Did he get promoted because he was Black? Did the *Times* give him second, third, and fourth chances because he was Black? Did the desire for diversity cause the problems at the *New York Times?*

Blair was not journalism's first liar. Ironically a week after Blair resigned, another famous fibber resurfaced, this time as the author of a new novel about a lying reporter. Stephen Glass was a 25-year-old writer for the *New Republic* when he decided to start making things up. Unlike Blair, who usually stole other people's reporting about real events, Glass invented entire news events and subjects to feature in the magazine. Among his most memorable creations were profiles of the First Church of George Herbert Walker Bush, a bond trading firm with a shrine to Alan Greenspan, and a conservative political conference overrun with drugs and sex. Not a word of any of it was true. Glass was finally caught in a made-for-TV moment when his editor demanded that the young reporter drive to the location of the political conference and reveal where supposedly sex-crazed participants snorted cocaine. Glass broke down in tears instead. But at the same time that Blair was being held up as proof that diversity does not work, Glass was doing interviews with *60 Minutes* pushing his first book.

Glass isn't the only example of a white reporter who was able to come back from a lie. Mike Barnicle, a popular columnist for the *Boston Globe,* was fired in 1998 for making up quotes. Within a year, he surfaced with a job as a columnist for the *New York Daily News.* He also has a TV gig with MSNBC as a pundit and often fills in for host Chris Mathews on the popular show *Hardball* when needed. Ruth Shalit, another former writer for the *New Republic* left under a plagiarism cloud in the mid-1990s and later went on to write for *GQ* and *Salon.* Elizabeth Wurtzel was fired by the *Dallas Morning News* for plagiarizing but that did not prevent her from later writing for *New York Magazine* and the *New Yorker.* She also penned the bestseller *Prozac Nation.* (Just for the sake of honest disclosure, Patricia Smith, a Black columnist, was dismissed from the *Globe* the same summer as Barnicle. She is a full-time poet and does no journalism now.)

The Blair coverage barely mentioned Barnicle et al. Instead, it was disgraced Black reporter Janet Cooke whose name often appeared. (A story on Blair in the conservative *Weekly Standard* simply ran under the headline "Janet Cooke Revisited.") In 1981, the *Washington Post* reporter was forced to give back the Pulitzer Prize she had received for the story about an 8-year-old heroin addict, after she confessed that little Jimmy existed only in her mind. That same year *New York Daily News* reporter Michael Daly was fired for a column he wrote about a British soldier in Northern Ireland when it was discovered the soldier didn't exist. Fifteen years after giving back her Pulitzer, Cooke was earning $6.15 an hour as a department store clerk in Kalamazoo, Michigan. Only weeks after leaving the *Daily News* in disgrace, Daly was hired by *New York Magazine.* By 1993, he was back at the *Daily News* where he continues to write today. (Blair eventually did land a book deal from Hollywood publishing house New Millennium Press, best know for unauthorized tomes on the O. J. Simpson trial and books on other made-for-television type scandals. Although Blair made it widely known throughout his own scandal that he wanted to write a book detailing his story, none of the traditional New York publishing houses would come near the disgraced reporter. Ironically, New Millennium filed for chapter 11 bankruptcy within days of announcing its deal with Blair.)

However, because Blair is Black, he is a symbol for all that is wrong with diversity. Generally, every news item on the scandal included an obligatory sentence about what this meant for newsroom diversity. He was proof that standards had to have been compromised in the name of diversity. At least that is what the media reported, and doesn't the media always tell the truth? For Black journalists, it was painful to go into newsrooms at that time. The cloud of suspicion was suffocating for all of us. A reporter friend of mine (not at the *Times*) was almost pushed to the edge by the constant questions from his white colleagues: Did you know him? Did you know Jayson?

The press coverage was relentless. The attacks on the *Times* were ruthless. In the end, the paper's top two editors—Howell Raines and Gerald Boyd—were forced to resign. Blair's actions had become much larger than just him. Diversity had come under such an attack because of the Blair affair that when Boyd (the highest-ranking African American in the paper's history) resigned, he felt the need to pledge his support for diversity.

Standing before a packed newsroom, atop a desk usually reserved for giving good news like the paper's latest Pulitzer Prize winnings, Boyd reached in his coat pocket for a slip of paper and read: "I stand for merit, not favoritism. I always have and always will. I stand for quality. Putting out the best newspaper one possibly can. I stand for inclusion, because I believe it makes us better. And I stand for diversity." At this point the editor was interrupted by applause from sections of the crowd. "I have spent my entire life embracing and working to make diversity matter, because it has to, and as long as I breathe I will continue on that path."[20]

Despite all the coverage that the Blair affair and its aftermath was receiving, Boyd's words got virtually no ink anywhere. The next day's coverage of the resignations almost exclusively focused on the downfall of top editor Raines and failed to spend much time on Boyd. An early wire piece by the Associated Press mentioned that Boyd declared his support for diversity but did not quote from his brief speech. Most news accounts, including the one in the *New York Times* the next day, did not mention Boyd's commitment to diversity at all.

Because the *Times* case is so extreme in its drama, the damage will probably be lasting. I tend to think, though, that it was just diversity's time, that it was vulnerable and Jayson Blair served as the last chink in the armor that allowed it to come under full attack as affirmative action had before. It's not surprising that the backlash coincided with a crippled economy still not fully recovered from the 9/11 terrorist attacks. When the diversity bashing was in full swing, the job market was in the midst of its longest hiring slump since the Depression. Wages had fallen behind inflation for most people, and workers were being asked to pay more of their health care costs. Because the economic pain was so widespread across class, color, region, and every other line, economists dubbed the rut the "egalitarian recession." [21] So, if not Blair, diversity would have been the fall guy to some other incident that the pack would have jumped on.

A sign that the wall was starting to crumble before Blair was that, leading up to the scandal, much of the criticism or disappointment with diversity was actually coming from supposed supporters of the cause. A recent study conducted by renowned management professor and HR scholar, Thomas A. Kochan, of the Massachusetts Institute of Technology's Sloan School of Management, bashes the business case of diversity to the core. When he started his 5-year study, Kochan did not intend to knock diversity. He set out to measure the impact of diversity on business results. He basically couldn't. Not because it isn't possible, but because even companies with well established and highly regarded diversity programs rarely conduct systematic analyses of the effects of their diversity efforts on the bottom line. In the end, Kochan concluded: "The diversity industry is built on sand."[22] And this is coming from the prodiversity camp.

More troubling than the fair-weather support of a single academic and the press that he may stir, is what actually led Kochan to that point. Why don't more companies directly link their diversity efforts to the bottom line? Business does not generally care about anything that is not tied to the bottom line. Any first-year MBA student will tell you that. The reality that corporate America has done no extensive research to put a dollar sign on the benefits of diversity, indicates that these initiatives may not be as dear to corporate hearts as we are led to believe. Without that kind of concrete evidence, these programs will always be marginalized, inherently weak, and vulnerable from every angle.

Take another case from my own industry, the media. (Because journalists like to write about themselves, their industry's diversity blunders tend to be harder to hide.) Faced with a dismal economy, Knight Ridder, the nation's third-largest newspaper company, began 2003 with a game for its managers: "The $100 Million Scavenger Hunt." That was the title of the memo sent to editors of its newspapers across the country asking them to help the company cut costs. The goal of the game was to slash $100 million from the Knight Ridder budget. This amount represented more than 4 percent of the newspaper company's operating costs of $2.24 billion. The memo offered a handful of suggestions as to where editors might find some cash—this being a scavenger hunt and all. Tips ranged from layoffs and department consolidations to pooling resources across the newspaper chain, which includes the *Philadelphia Inquirer* and *Miami Herald* among its papers. Without fanfare, or explanation, another suggestion was to cut diversity initiatives.[23] This fuels this generation's cynicism about corporate commitment on issues of race.

When the internal memo was leaked to the *New York Times*, the surprised reaction in corporate circles was more focused on its flippant nature—the scavenger hunt premise of the suggestions—than on the suggestions themselves—including the proposal to cut diversity initiatives. What makes it worse is that this industry is already struggling to reach minimum diversity goals. In 1978, after discovering that minorities represented only 4 percent of the nation's journalists, the American Society of Newspaper Editors issued an industrywide goal for newsrooms to mirror the diversity of the nation by 2000. As the industry approached the millennium, it was so far behind in meeting its goal that the ASNE gave themselves an extra 25 years to get there. In 2002, people of color made up only 12.5 percent of newspaper staffs, falling short of the goal of 31 percent and being only 1 percent higher than the year before. Looks like a 2025 deadline might be cutting it close. It is disturbing that even in an industry outspoken about diversifying itself, Knight Ridder's recommendation to cut such programs did not draw a single whisper of outrage, much less disappointment. Such corporate moves are expected, but that does not mean that they should be accepted.

The post-civil rights generation has good reason to be cynical. After watching the definition of diversity get so diluted, this generation, always on the lookout for empty promises, has developed a healthy skepticism about diversity's value to corporate America. That skepticism is part of their cynicism, which is also rooted in the frustration and betrayal that this generation shares from fighting demons that you can't always see. Now, diversity is in danger of becoming the latest empty promise.

Which brings us back to Lisa, the HR diversity chair, and her declaration that race was sacrificed on the altar of diversity. "Diversity has to leave out race for it to be valued in corporate America," she says. "Any diversity person will say we don't just look at race—we look at a number of factors. This tells you they've discounted race." Lisa's criticism of the diversity movement always struck me. For a high-ranking HR executive, it seemed like career suicide. For a Black woman, it verged on heresy. For a believer in the true goals of diversity, it must have hurt. But it is also something that needed to be said. Diversity, in today's watered-down, one-size-fits-all form, is flawed.

Knocking something that you ultimately support is dangerous because no one ever listens long enough to hear the explanation or nuances. The indictment stands, painted with a massive brush stroke that is impossible to wash away. But my criticism here is not with the ultimate goal or theory of diversity, but the application.

This generation sees those flaws, and it makes them uneasy with the issue. This generation believes that race is important. They have learned this from experience—from surviving the affirmative action warfare when they were teenagers to Working While Black as young professionals to the glass ceilings that this highly credentialed group still faces today. For the post-civil rights generation, there is no doubt that race still matters.

"I'm a Black woman on Wall Street—Of course, I think about race every single day," says Erica, the ex-trader at J.P. Morgan. "I wouldn't be able to survive if I didn't."

Logically, race shouldn't really matter anymore given this generation's success. Our parents dreamed that it wouldn't. Those who stared down fire hoses and others who clenched their fists must have believed that, at some level, race didn't have to matter. Equality included color blindness. But race is not logical, it is emotional. So it didn't work out that way.

That is why diversity as an ideal is important to them. Equally, it is also why a definition of diversity that belittles the significance of race is hard to swallow. At the same time, that the success of diversity is directly related to the movement's ability to belittle race also hurts. All of those issues will affect this generation of Black professionals although at this point exactly how they may be affected is still undefined. There's an underlying uneasiness, like a queasiness in the pit of their stomachs. They know how important race is even if the environment they work in constantly skirts the issue or deals with it indirectly. There is no comfortable coexistence between the two. The friction is constant. How this generation deals with such discomfort will be interesting. Furthermore, if race continues to be the focus of one segment of the office while everyone else overlooks it, what does that mean for relations around the watercooler?

On the most tangible level, the future of diversity in the workplace is at stake because of this discomfort. This time it is the goal, not the application. Black executives are still corporate America's most powerful minority group. Compared with the other ethnic minorities, African Americans have gone farther with more people. So if Black executives lose faith, can these programs survive? And if they do survive after that faith is lost, what does that say about Black corporate clout? Either way, the situation is not good.

Two years ago when I first tried to write about the diversity hoax, I just wanted to expose the secret. After talking to the Orals and Susans and Alvins and Seans, though, I realized I wasn't the only skeptic. Such skepticism can be dangerous—sometimes it leads you to places you didn't intend to visit. Is diversity ultimately doomed? Let's hope not. Maybe the challenge is simply reeling in the definition of diversity to make it meaningful again. There is value in doing a few things well instead of trying to do everything, maybe not so well. We don't need another McPizza. Race is already sitting at the table, so stop ignoring it. Despite the best efforts of the Bureau of the Census and its multicultural boxes, race is not going away any time soon. True there are signs that younger generations might be starting to think about these issues differently. Then again, they are still checking a box and that means they are still thinking about race.

It is time for the American workplace to take race seriously. No more hiding. No more innuendos. No more double-sided politeness. No more damn indirectness. That is the first step.

More difficult perhaps is the next step. Skepticism can be tough to break away from. It can impede productivity, stifle desires, kill ambition, and damage just about anything that makes people succeed. But, if this post-civil rights generation is truly supportive of diversity—the goal, not the application—as they claim to be, then they are going to have to learn how to believe. Otherwise, the fight might as well be over, and diversity by any definition will definitely have lost.

For skeptics and members of the post-civil rights generation who are trying to climb the ladder, believing is hard. But it had to be said. Thank you, Lisa.

5

GENERATIONAL WARFARE

When I was coming up my grandmother would say things like "be a credit to your race." Each and every one of us somehow carried the entire reputation of African Americans in America on our shoulders as we left the community and went out into the world. This generation doesn't have that burden. Now, no one tells [them] those things because it is just passé.

—Richard D. Parsons, CEO Time Warner

When I am one of only a few African Americans at a Princeton, or in corporate America, or any situation I always feel that I am not just representing me. If I don't succeed then the next brother or sister might not get the opportunity. Why do I have to carry this responsibility in 2003? It doesn't matter why, I just do, we all do.

—Bill Jordan, 30, vice president, Wells Fargo

T hese two quotes say it all. The End. Next chapter. Tempting, but let's get serious . . .

Not to sound crazy, but sometimes the people I interview start to have conversations in my head. Bill Jordan and Dick Parsons were chitchatting in my mind for weeks. Bill has never met Parsons, and the CEO of Time Warner is probably not used to sharing the podium with a young VP still trying to prove himself. Still, that didn't stop them, the two generations, from talking, if only in my head. When it comes to the two generations—the groundbreakers and the post-civil rights babies—these two quotes say it all.

And someone's not listening.

It happens in every family. Kids versus Parents is as age-old as Cain versus Abel. So, there is also friction between the generations of Black professionals. Exactly who appears not to be listening will depend on which side of the line you are standing on.

To the groundbreakers, the current generation has it easy, with nothing to complain about. Nothing that this generation is going through can be as difficult as the groundbreaker

109

experience of being the Firsts. Thoughts of "If I made it, everyone can" run rampant. It sounds harmless, but this frustration can fester. One day I was interviewing Tom Jones, the former Cornell revolutionary who is now sitting at the top of Citigroup, about the ceilings he has managed to break through. I made the mistake of nodding my head in agreement as he recounted the racist difficulties of being the first Black face to reach each spot on his résumé. The nod prompted him to lecture me, and the rest of my generation, for not taking advantage of all that we have been given.

The current crop of Black professionals doesn't find things that easy. So they immediately put groundbreakers on a shelf labeled "out-of-date" when they start talking about all the progress that has been made. Such talk prompts this generation to accuse the groundbreakers of becoming satisfied and complacent, or even of turning their back once they've made it instead of helping those who are still coming up.

Two months after Gerald Boyd was forced to step down as managing editor of the *New York Times* because of the fallout from Jayson Blair, the newspaper executive surfaced at the annual convention of the National Association of Black Journalists. Speaking publicly for the first time since the scandal, Boyd wanted to make one thing clear. Contrary to what the media coverage had implied, he was *not* Blair's mentor. "Some have suggested that I looked the other way because Jayson is Black," said Boyd, standing on an empty stage before a packed hotel ballroom in Dallas. "That is absolutely untrue. . . . While I have always been proud of my heritage as an African American and have proudly and successfully worked to promote all kinds of diversity, absolutely no one can peg me as some newsroom racial revolutionary." Commenting on the speculation that senior management reportedly did not come to him with concerns about Blair because both are Black, he added, "I was not the

Black managing editor, I was the managing editor." The crowd cheered, giving Boyd, one of the nation's top Black journalists, two enthusiastic standing ovations. But one issue still bothered the post-civil rights babies in the room: "I was wanting to know why someone in his position *didn't* mentor Blair," asked Deron Snyder, a sports columnist for the *News-Press* of Fort Myers, Florida, after Boyd's remarks.[1] This, too, is the type of frustration that rumbles and festers.

When it comes to race, these are real differences between the two generations that are not so much age specific but truly generational. It is no secret that the old and the young often see the same things differently. But those age-specific views are temporary and exist primarily because the viewers are either young or old. For example, invincibility is a belief of youth. When people are young, death does not seem like a real possibility, consequences don't seem forever, and lack of experience allows them to think they are always right. Eighteen-year-old drivers can be reckless because they don't think they can be killed or even injured in an accident, whereas 48-year-olds are usually more cautious because visions of invincibility faded years ago. But the half-empty/half-full differences between the post-civil rights generation and the groundbreakers, as illustrated by all those festering frustrations, are due not to age but to a generational gap. The opposing views of these two groups transcend age and each generation sticks with its own. For instance, the Beyond Rage mentality sprouts from being the children of the frustrated— just as depression babies hid money in their mattresses for the rest of their lives. The mentality that comes from those shared experiences will not change with age; instead it unites a generation. Beyond Rage is a defining lens that the post-civil rights generation will forever see through. Hence the gap is a generational rift.

Truth is, both generations are blinded. The groundbreakers can't see past how much the world has changed and the post-civil rights generation can't see past the change still needed. And both sides are frustrated with each other's blindness.

This is why Parsons and Bill, the generations, were talking in my head.

Bill, 30, is still in the early stages of his career. After graduating from Princeton, he spent 5 years in the nonprofit world working for the foundation arm of the Black mutual fund group Ariel Capital Management. But, with a Kim-like epiphany that the business world was the better venue to uplift the race, he traded in the nonprofit sector for business school and ended up at the real estate investment arm of Wells Fargo. "To make more than small strides, I figured I better educate myself in the language of business." When our paths crossed, he had been in the corporate world only two years. Despite his short tenure, he had already melded his empowerment intentions and corporate success in true Black Power Inc. fashion. Like Kim at Dell, or Richard at Booz, Bill's business success was very much a mission. The business aspects and his social views about what is best for the race were blended, wrapped up together, and intertwined. The career becomes the movement. In fact, Bill chose real estate investment because of its ability to transform and uplift communities. "I want to take what I learn in corporate America and use it to impact the lives of those [Black folks] that don't have an opportunity," says Bill explaining that he had no intention of forever using his MBA to make "rich clients richer" (sounds like the Blackprint). Bill, being a true post-civil rights revolutionary, though, quickly adds: "But do it with a for-profit mentality. That is how I can make the most difference."

Bill grew up in the cornfields of Belleville, Illinois. His dad is a retired air force pilot and Mom raised four children full time. Belleville is as close to the Jim Crow era as a post-civil rights baby can get. In the early 1990s, *60 Minutes* profiled the scenic, tree-lined town as a symbol of racial friction. When Bill was growing up, the town of 44,000 people had fewer than 40 Black residents. In his elementary school of 600 children, there were only 4 Black faces; one belonged to his brother.

The friction comes from the border the white town shares with predominantly Black and poor East St. Louis, Missouri. Go-back-to-Africa. Go-back-to-East-St.-Louis. N-I-G-G-E-R: Bill heard such racial threats and taunts a lot when he was growing up. For him, race became a reality at the age of 7. He was cutting the grass of his front lawn when a group of local teenagers pounced. From a child's viewpoint, he looked up and all he could see were the faces. The circle of heads bending over him blocked out the sun. The ring of twisted mouths shouted for 5 minutes, 10 minutes, who-knows-how-many minutes hurling racial epithets. Then one by one, they spit in his face. In a moment, the crowd was gone. Thinking back on the incident, Bill squirms and tries hard not to unlock the feelings of the 7-year-old from his memory. But that it all actually happened is not what now disturbs him the most. He is more disturbed by the fact that it didn't faze him *then*. At the time, he just wiped his face and kept on mowing. It was Belleville. It was Black life in a white world, even for a 7-year-old. Twenty-three years later, as Bill tells the story to a listener with pen, pad, and tape recorder in hand documenting the incident in history, he wipes his face, as if he still can't get it clean.

Despite the civil-rights era setting of his childhood, Bill still has a very post-civil rights viewpoint of life. That is why when Bill and his Dad talk about issues of Blackness—they argue.

"My Dad's focus is white racism," starts Bill, as if revealing family secrets. We both sit back in the chairs in my office, as if in therapy. "That is not my concern. Let's work on things we *can* control. If so-and-so isn't going to hire me because I'm Black, I'm not going to change that. I just can't. What we can change is making sure we have the skills to turn into money and empower ourselves. The laws are changed, the neighborhood is changed, desegregation is changed. How much are you going to fight for someone to give you opportunity? It's time to move on. I accept that I have to be twice as good."

The session was over, but Bill had revealed a lot. The Beyond Rage mantra, of course, I'd heard before, a lot. But Bill, with his tone, his sighs, and his borderline rant, also gave me a glimpse into the frustration that still exists—not with white America, but with Black. His frustration is not that of a son with his dad (although that probably makes it easier to see), his frustration is that of a post-civil rights baby with the previous generation.

"I love my Dad, love talking to my Dad," says Bill. "But I argue with my Dad about these things a lot."

And that's the problem.

Armed with Bill's voice in my head, I sat down with Dick Parsons to find out just what one of the most powerful Black executives in the United States thought about my generation. For the next crop of young Black executives, the Time Warner CEO is a role model. His name constantly pops up—always with much respect and always with a bit of awe. Parsons generates a curiosity of the kind usually reserved for magicians. How did he do that? Pull a rabbit out of his hat or become CEO—both tricks are a mystery. Susan, the ambassador, once said to me that if Dick Parsons leaves his office, goes home at night, and simply puts his feet up, too tired to do anything else, that's okay. This is the awe factor at work. Although this generation is constantly critical of those executives who seem not to be doing enough for Black America, with Parsons it almost doesn't matter how much or little he does because young professionals are frozen by the "how did he do that" question. Alvin, from Sony, offers Parsons as the only role model for the career he'd like to have. As in, Alvin, what job do you want? "To run a multimedia empire, like Dick Parsons."

So Parsons looms large. Ken Chenault, who as CEO of American Express has been in the CEO seat a little longer, is another name that pops up almost as often as Parsons. The two names are usually linked like a tandem bike. In fact, when Susan was saying that it is okay if Parsons is tired, she did not forget to extend the pardon to Ken Chenault, too. There are others who have reached the top. Franklin Raines is CEO of Fannie Mae, but because of the nature of his business—the quasi-public status of securing mortgages—he is undeservedly often overlooked by this young crowd. Bob Johnson, founder of BET, became a billionaire when he sold the company to Viacom. He is revered for his entrepreneurship and deal-making skills, but he doesn't get the how-did-he-do-that stare. Farther down in people's minds is Stan O'Neal, CEO of Merrill Lynch. Outside Wall Street, he does not seem to immediately spring to mind for this wave of Black executives, but perhaps that has more to do with the perception, right or wrong, that he is more reluctant to embrace issues of race. The bottom line is that Parsons and Chenault are seen as conquerors of a system and they won without losing their Blackness.

Raised in Brooklyn and Queens, Richard D. Parsons admits he never wanted to be a CEO when he was growing up. Chief legal counsel of the NAACP Legal Defense fund and then the Supreme Court, like Thurgood Marshall, was what he envisioned. It was the law—legal barriers and collapses—that was changing the world and that is what he was drawn to. In 1971, he had the highest score in the state on the New York Bar exam. The Rockefellers then promptly scooped him up to work in the governor's office and to serve as the family's personal attorney. He enjoyed a coveted legal career in conservative circles eventually following Nelson Rockefeller to the Ford administration, where Parsons ran the domestic policy council. When the Republicans were voted out of office, Parsons returned to a legal career in New York at the prestigious white shoe firm of Patterson, Belknap, Webb & Tyler, where he was a managing partner. When he eventually left law for business, he took on the CEO post at troubled Dime Savings Bank in New York, one of the largest thrift institutions in the nation. Even though he had no banking experience, he managed to hold off regulators by raising $300 million in new capital and ultimately merged Dime with another thrift bank in 1994.[2] The next year he was tapped to be president of Time Warner, where he had already been on the board since 1991. Despite continuing to move into key leadership positions after the media company's merger with AOL, Parsons remained under the radar of observers, and many were stunned when he was named CEO in 2002.

In person, it is easy to forget that Parsons is a big-time CEO. And that is a good thing. Perched at the very top of the ladder, he still manages to come across as a nice guy with a down-to-earth charm that makes others, even the most awkward and unconfident, feel comfortable. So we talked freely, openly, and unapologetically—the corporate titan and the post-civil rights baby—about being Black.

For the record, Parsons is a "Me Too" executive—one of those 40+-year-olds—clearly of a different generation than the current one—who huff and puff about being post-civil rights babies, too. Parsons, 54, tried to claim the post-civil rights name tag while spitting out stories of marches and protests and dogs and fire hoses during his teenage years. For me, his memory was enough to say he is *not* post-civil rights material. Post-civil rights babies were born after the hoses were turned

116

off. That world is not one they remember; it is one they were taught about. And that's a big difference. But Parsons (and other Me Toos) said that since those memories were from his childhood, not when he came of age and developed, he qualifies as post. Then, showing off his famous reputation for the art of compromise, he suggested that he is a member of the first post-civil rights generation and I belong to the second. We agreed to disagree on who staked claim to the label. It wasn't the only thing we would disagree about.

In a nutshell, Parsons told me that compared with his own generation, the next is "more secure, smarter, better educated, and less inhibited by their own insecurities or lack of confidence. You are more citizens of the world than we were."

For Parsons, one of this generation's biggest advantages is that, in the most simplistic terms, it doesn't have the burden of race. That is what "citizens of the world" means. "You guys are better equipped as citizens of the world as opposed to just African Americans whose first calling card is I'm African American and that is who I am. Your first calling card is I'm a competent person." Dropping the African American calling card is what post-civil rights is supposed to mean, after all. In contrast, Parsons sees his generation as thinking of themselves as Black first and not much more. He thinks the overemphasis on race is really a cover-up, overcompensating for the generation's own insecurities in the wider world. (That is why "citizens of the world" is the highest of praise.)

Parsons believes the problem with the Black calling card mentality is that it takes away options. This is where we started to disagree—I as a representative of Bill and the post-civil rights generation, and he as spokesperson for himself, Bill's Dad, and the groundbreakers. Parsons argues that people end up less willing to take risks if they are always concerned with putting the best face forward for the race. Taking a risk, traveling a path not usually taken, or doing something unexpected, all have the possibility of failing. And if that failure is not just the individual's but all of Black America's, the person will avoid taking those risks. By always thinking about what is best for the race first, he argues, Black folks won't try anything new. Ultimately, though, it is the new things waiting to be tried that will be the best for the race.

The CEO's favorite "statement of philosophy" comes from Woody Allen: "Eighty percent of success is showing up." He uses it a lot. He says the danger with race is some use it as an excuse for not "showing up." Why strive to be a cross-country skier, or a performance artist, or even an astronaut—if Black folks don't do such things. But Parsons' entire career is built on things that people have told him Black folks can't do. When he was the personal attorney for the Rockefeller family, when he abruptly left law for business, when he took over as CEO (at Dime) in an industry he had absolutely no experience in, even when he won the crown at AOL Time Warner (as it was then called)—these were all things Black folks weren't supposed to be able to do.

"I remember in the mid-1970s someone was telling me how the real world was as they saw it," says Parsons. "They told me 'you can be a lawyer for the [Rockefeller] family, you can do this, or that, but they are never going to put a Black person in charge of the money. They aren't going to put *you* in charge of the money. You will never be in charge of the Rockefeller Foundation.'" Parsons didn't buy it. In 1979, Franklin Thomas became the first Black president of the Ford Foundation, and Parsons still feels vindicated.

To his credit, Parsons has faith that anything can happen. He lives by it. Because he feels it so strongly, he is never afraid to at least try something new. "It never occurred to me that I couldn't [*fill in the blank here*]," he says. "I always believed that I could do or be whatever I chose to if I really put my mind to it." He thinks that this attitude is not shared by most of his generation but is held by mine. Indeed, his proclamation that it never occurred to him that he, as a Black man, couldn't do something, immediately reminded me of Alvin at Sony and his mantra: He "expects to win, period" as a Black man.

For Parsons, this all adds up to one thing: This generation is more inclined to show up. In his mind, this generation inherently shows up because it does not have all those "society imposed limitations [about race] hardwired into [its] thinking." Meaning, he sees race as a nonissue for the post-civil rights generation, which he argues has not been programmed to think that they can't do something because they are Black. They have been taught to think they can do anything. As a result, they show up for everything. This is a major advantage—or 80 percent of success.

Hmmm. The difference is that this generation doesn't see wearing a Black face as a burden, or as a weight. Instead it is a necessary obligation. Bill doesn't ask why, he just *carries*. This generation takes risks because they carry that weight, not because they are free from it. The post-civil rights generation succeeds because they are Black. Their Blackness is what drives them and what pushes them, and ultimately it becomes their goal to succeed for the race that they are carrying. They want a new and different outcome, not the one they were handed—so they try new things.

This is a wide disconnect. Parsons thinks it is a difference in age—the impatience of youth, he says. I think that it is a true gap between generations. Maybe my youthful impatience prevents me from seeing that the feelings of my generation may fade away at some time in the future. The behavior of this generation, though, is a direct reaction to what they've already seen and a concerted effort to change things. More important

119

than whether these differences are a gap or simply a disconnect, is that the differences exist at all. That is truly the hurdle that needs to be overcome.

This rift, this generation gap in thinking, causes talk about being lucky to creep up. The groundbreakers see all the progress and cannot help but think the next generation is lucky. How could we not be? "Dr. King could never have been hired by a Fortune 500 company;" says Bruce Gordon, 57, President of Verizon, from his corner office one day. Gordon, one of the highest-ranking Black executives in the telecom industry, is in charge of Verizon's $25 billion retail markets division. "Not because he didn't have the talent, but because he never would have been given the chance." Very true. Getting a better starting point *is* lucky, and this generation has the best starting point so far. A white, male colleague once asked me: If I could pick any period in history, which one would I want to live in? Coworkers around the watercooler had picked everything from ancient Rome to colonial America to Babe Ruth's 1927 season. My answer was: None. As a Black woman, why would I *ever* want to live in the past—life would only be harder. So it is completely understandable that the groundbreakers are stuck on the fact that this generation has things better. Parsons, himself, is almost giddy talking about how "lucky" I am. Imagine the possibilities! This is progress! This is good! His excitement over my generation's ability to show up is sincere. He thinks we're lucky, and he's not the only one. Parsons; Bill's Dad; Tom Jones, when he's annoyed with my nodding; the Me Toos—they all think this generation is lucky. And that means one thing: We have no excuses.

With all that luck, how could we ever have a legitimate excuse for anything? Parsons interrupts his giddy talk only to let me know that he "hates excuse making." The groundbreakers give off the sense that any excuses are somewhat disrespectful after they have managed to achieve success against all odds. That is why Jones, the powerful Citigroup executive, lectured me for my nodding. We will never have it as tough. Never! Things aren't perfect, but they sure are a lot better. True. So we'd better realize the power of our lucky place. True. Otherwise what is the point? Exactly.

The "lucky" and "no excuses" pairing can lead to resentment or, at the very least, some general head shaking. To say a person is lucky belittles his or her accomplishments, even if unintentionally. In schoolyard jargon, it is called a "head start." Whenever someone gets a head start, it is not a legitimate win. Those are the rules. The post-civil rights generation doesn't like to hear that they are lucky, even if they are. No, scratch that. The post-civil rights babies know they are lucky, but they don't want to hear it. It is like acknowledging that their parents are right. So, yes, there is some cockiness there, some impatience, and at times even some youth-filled bravado.

But most of all, the post-civil rights generation doesn't want to hear that because of such luck they have no excuses. First and foremost, they believe that they are offering not excuses but the truth. They just want to be heard, spreading the truth. If what they are saying is characterized as an excuse, they take it as a sign that they are not being heard—or worse—that no one is listening.

This generation has legitimate gripes when it comes to being heard. Their voices are often drowned out by the shouts of the groundbreakers from above and the Black mass below. In the scheme of issues, the problems of young Black professionals—the generation of the most successful Black folks, ever—doesn't rank too high on the list of emergencies. But it doesn't mean that those problems should be ignored.

The excuses criticism is a reminder that, again, they are not being heard. The bottom line is the two generations see things differently. Maybe they should. Still, there is a gap, a rift, a split, and it is an unnecessary division. That is the point.

Many weeks after the night Bill and I had our therapy session in my office, I got an e-mail from him. He wanted to talk again. He was thinking about a question I had asked: whether there had been any turning points in his life that triggered a change in his views on race. He came up with three. The e-mail read: 1. The N-Word and college football teammates. 2. Trip to Africa and Africans' outlook on how African Americans affect the Diaspora. 3. Realization that "everybody that is your color is not your kind."

The third bullet really caught my attention. To protect the guilty, Bill insisted that the who, what, where, and when of this last story not get out there for people to read. Since the incident, involving a dinner on the road with coworkers, would be too identifiable, I agreed. But the details are not what matter. The moral of the third turning point is that there is tremendous diversity among Black folks, which means that not everyone thinks about things the same way. Or, most importantly, thinks Black first.

For Bill, with his Belleville childhood, not thinking Black first was a major revelation. That lesson is powerful. To discover that every Black face may not be as committed as he is to all Black faces was a big deal. When you feel you are constantly carrying the weight, it is somewhat jarring to realize that not everyone finds it necessary to hold a part of the load. On some intellectual level, it is an obvious truth. But on an emotional level, it can still stop you in your tracks. When something is that important, it is easy to forget that it may not be important to everyone. Navigating the corporate world showed Bill that even if people are committed, there are many ways to express that commitment. More important, just because we may all be heading for the same finish line doesn't mean everyone is going to agree on the best route. Bill's third bullet acknowledges his realization that some of his fellow executives take questionable paths. It is also interesting that it took working in corporate America for Bill to learn this lesson. It reinforces that it is work where issues of race get shaped. He wasn't the only one learning such lessons.

Without a shred of concrete evidence beyond his gut feeling, one 34-year-old senior finance manager on Wall Street was convinced that the post-civil rights generation would more readily extend their hand to other Black folks (specifically in hiring) than the groundbreaker generation has ever done. His matter-of-fact tone was what was so startling about the critique. "They are too busy breaking down doors to be concerned with the rest of us," he said half-joking.

It was one of those comments that sting. Did he really say that? The words were striking, although the meaning wasn't. The resentment that he alluded to I had heard about before. Criticisms of those who don't do enough are common. Coded slights of the previous generation are nothing new either. But I had never heard the critique wrapped in that kind of package before. The pairing of knocking down doors with not having time for those who followed is hard to swallow. It is an interesting mix of warped logic and legitimate complaint. Isn't breaking down doors enough? If not, maybe breaking down doors shouldn't be the goal. The flippancy of the critique hints at the dissatisfaction with the state of things now, when doors are supposedly open. Such dissatisfaction is what makes criticism of a generation obsessed with breaking down doors even possible.

After thinking it over, it occurred to me that this post-civil rights executive was really complaining about masks. It was the same lesson that Bill was learning when he realized that there are those who do not think Black first. Black faces who get to the top and then disassociate themselves from any and all Black faces behind them are public enemy number one to this generation. This generation's measure of success is based in what it means for Black folks. That is the Blackprint that they constantly follow. If someone can't even extend a hand to Black folks within their own company, then their "success" is meaningless. This generation is not afraid to congregate, doesn't close their doors, and refuses to compromise who they are. So success without extending a hand back is not only meaningless, it's in the way of progress, just as a teammate who doesn't pull his weight is in the way. So the criticism is not so much about the time and energy it takes to break down doors, but about what gets sacrificed to break those doors down. If the sacrifice is race, then for this generation, it is simply not worth it.

Because the post-civil rights generation rejects masks, this finance executive concluded, "We will do much better. We are not as afraid." For him, the different starting points that the two generations were coming from were precisely why one would go out of the way to hire Black faces whereas the other would not. The groundbreakers were thankful to be where they were because they knew it could be worse; the post-civil rights generation was dissatisfied because they knew it could be better.

I could see his point. Still, neither generation fully understood where the other was coming from, and that I couldn't overlook. There was a connection inherently missing at the root of the head-nodding lectures, lucky talk, and door-opening sarcasm. The journalist in me still needed to learn more. So I headed downtown to find out what Ken Chenault, the CEO of American Express, thought of all this—race and the generations.

Hailing from Long Island, the middle-class suburbs of New York, Chenault's background mirrors more closely that of the post-civil rights generation than that of his peers. The son of a dentist, Chenault is a product of private schools, tony Bowdoin College in Maine, and Harvard Law School. At Bowdoin in the early 1970s, the small group of Black students would get into intellectual debates over whether African Americans should work within the system or outside it to effect change. Chenault, one of the few Black students who freely mingled and felt comfortable at any table in the cafeteria (white or Black), definitely defended the in-the-system side.[3] After Harvard, he had a brief stint in consulting before ending up at American Express in 1981. The executive built a reputation as the consummate insider with the outsider's eye. He would steer away from some prestigious assignments in favor of having the greatest impact by turning around the truly down-and-out departments.[4] In 2001, after serving 4 years in the number two spot, he was named CEO.

Chenault manages to be smooth and confident in an unpretentious way. There is an intensity about him that radiates intelligence and focus. He is not afraid to sit back for a moment of silence and think about what he wants to say. It is amazing how rare a move like that is in interviews. Most people shoot off answers to questions immediately as if they know every answer no matter what the question might be. Chenault gives the impression that he is constantly thinking.

An entry-level executive ran into Chenault one day in the hallways of American Express soon after he was named CEO. The post-civil rights baby did not hesitate to ask the new CEO if there was anything he missed about the life he had before being at the top of the corporate food chain. Chenault paused and thought about it. Weeks later in a crowded elevator, Chenault saw the young Black executive again. The CEO leaned over and whispered that he had come up with two things he missed. The young executive didn't mind that Chenault refused to reveal what the two things were. He was just stunned that the CEO had taken the time to think about his passing question.

When I met with Chenault, I was at the end of my research. I kept getting word that he was eager to talk, but securing a spot on his calendar proved to be almost as hard as it is for the Mets to win a game. I had just about given up when his office called with a date. By the time we sat down at his office overlooking Ground Zero, I had been talking and talking with people about these issues for a long time. I hate to admit it, but I was at a point where there were few surprises in what people had to say. So I went in expecting to disagree with most things Chenault had to say, in much the same way my conversations with Parsons and other groundbreakers had proceeded. But I was surprised.

In one short interview, Chenault was blowing away my generalizations about the generations. He wasn't saying what he was supposed to say. Instead, he was talking about the importance of race, obligation to the race, and about Blacks succeeding without compromising their Blackness. He was making me pause and think.

"It is critical for African Americans to be clear about who you are," says Chenault who repeated this theme often during our chat. "If you are not clear about your identity people can sense that and will end up taking advantage of you."

Wow. This is exactly how the post-civil rights generation is trying to live. This *is* Beyond Rage. Chenault also talked about all the opportunities that my generation now has, how things are better, and how far we've come. "The reality is the opportunities are far more substantial than they have been in our history." But there was no mention of this generation being lucky. Instead, like the post-civil rights generation, he was more concerned with all the climbing that still needed to be done. "I think at the end of the day I am encouraged by the attitude [of the next generation] and some of the early signs of progress. But the reality is the next 10 years will tell if we are able to build on those early successes. What is going to be most important is the criteria that we use. What will be critical is that we are not just seeing representation improve in the CEO level but it is very important to see representation dramatically improve in the senior management and middle management level because that is where we'll know progress has been sustained."

But wait, that was not supposed to be his focus. Chenault was not supposed to be saying things like "your identity [race] is critical." He was not supposed to be agreeing with Bill that Black folks need to focus on things that they can control. "People have followed my leadership throughout my tenure here," he says of his experience at American Express as a Black executive. "That is not to say that I haven't heard about some people who have had some issues. They are not going to come out in front in a corporate setting. But that is the reality. How do you fully control that? I don't think you can. But what you can control is your performance, your relationships, and your behaviors."

Now I was the one thinking. Could I have been wrong? Was there really no generational shift? Were the generations much closer in their viewpoints about race than I had thought? After all those conversations, though, all that talking, talking, talking, I don't think so. I realized that Chenault did not blow away my theory at all. He represents just one grain of sand that shifted differently than the rest of the beach. Generalizations are not an exact science. Besides, look where that one grain is now. Here was a 51-year-old groundbreaker driven by the same philosophy that now drives the post-civil rights generation—that race matters, so don't apologize. If his biggest piece of advice to the post-civil rights generation, or "young African Americans" as he likes to say, is to be proud of your race and who you are or you can't succeed (this is his advice), then I'll take it. I'll take it because this 51-year-old groundbreaking executive made it all the way to CEO. Chenault is proof that Beyond Rage works.

Also, if the sands can shift at different rates, then the generational rift does not have to be permanent. Maybe there can be fluidity when it comes to the generations and their Blackness. And that's a good thing.

This reminded me of the first time I ever spoke with Dick Parsons—he had been CEO of AOL Time Warner for 5 days. We talked about race and about being a Black CEO. Five days into the new job, and race was all over the headlines. There wasn't a story around that didn't "out" Parsons as a Black man by at least the end of the first paragraph. He was gracious and tolerant of my questions but admitted that he thought all the emphasis on Black instead of CEO was "annoying." A little more than a year later when I sat down with Parsons again to talk about the generation that is hoping to step into his shoes, his views on race had noticeably changed. Race *was* important, at least more important than he had thought.

"Many people have written in the abstract that race is the quintessential question in America. I used to reject it out of hand because I thought it was so silly. But I'm beginning to think that they were right. . . . We just can't seem to get past it." That is Parsons, the man.

And Parsons, the executive: "I think I and probably some of our managers here don't spend enough time thinking about the complexion of the workforce. We have an affirmative burden to think about race though."

For a man to go from dubbing the public's emphasis on race as "annoying" to calling it the nation's quintessential issue a year later is an interesting and substantial arc. It is more interesting that this shift happened after the man had reached the very top of the corporate world, CEO of one of the biggest and most influential companies in the nation. I took it as a sign that color blindness really is meaningless. But by acknowledging the true importance race did make, Parsons seemed to be more post-civil rights (the second generation), if only for a moment.

So this is where the discussion between Bill and Parsons, the generations, stops getting heated, in my mind.

The generations must keep talking, though, or they will continue to drift apart. The distance is a harmful distraction and does a great job of slowing progress down. In truth, both sides are right, and wrong. Neither is giving the other generation credit. There is value in opening doors. It allows Beyond Rage to stand on firm ground and even be possible. Succeeding—making sure the group continues to climb—once those doors are open is not easy either. Each link in the chain is necessary. The generations must unite and stop fighting over slices when the whole pie is what matters.

Something was still nagging me. If Parsons didn't pass on his grandmother's advice—to be a credit to the race—what did he teach his post-civil rights children instead? "Don't walk on the furniture, don't talk with your mouth full," he says laughing. Seriously? "We told them to be a credit to themselves." There was also one bit of advice the CEO did pass down. "One thing I did tell them that my mom used to tell me all the time is the world doesn't owe you a living."

"I heard a great expression once." Parsons lounged back; his 6-foot-4-inch frame was stretched to its fullest. He began to spin a tale, one generation to the next. He told me about a time when he was stuck in a crowd of people. Someone in the crowd, talking to everyone and no one, was complaining about how unfair life was, about how no one would give Black folks a break, "blah, blah, blah." Finally, from deep in the crowd, a woman shouted back, "Get off the cross, we need the wood." Tale spun. "It's a good expression," he added. I nodded (lecture-free this time) and smiled. And not because the CEO had cranked up his voice in his best old lady, crab-apple imitation to utter the "get off the cross" advice. Back in his own voice, Parsons continued: "There are enough people out there to persecute you. You don't need to persecute yourself. So, go give it a shot."

I smiled because that was one thing we agreed on.

6

THIS GENERATION NEEDS NO LEADERS

The first step for Black folks is realizing that there is not going to be a leader and there isn't any movement—unless you count economics.

—Shawn Baldwin, 36, founder and CEO of
Capital Management Group Securities

I have Jesse Jackson to thank for leading me to Shawn. We met at a press conference for the Rainbow PUSH Coalition's Wall Street Project—the annual conference that Jackson holds to focus attention on diversity on Wall Street. Rev. Jackson was wowing the media with his latest antiracism sound bites. The winner this time: "We didn't know how good baseball could be until everybody could play. We don't know how good our economy can be until everybody can participate." Shawn, who heads his own money management firm, was part of the crowd of supporters standing behind the civil rights leader on the stage. Just what was this post-civil rights baby doing there?

Shawn, the son of a supervisor at the telephone company back in Dayton, Ohio, is the boy our mothers would say has had good home training. He opens doors, takes a woman's coat, bows his head before every meal, and sends off thank-you notes after get-togethers. The investment banker also drops rap lyrics as easily as market advice.

His speech is sprinkled with old school platitudes, things *grandmama and 'em* used to say: "It is better to die on your feet then live on your knees." That one was my favorite. The Baldwin family truth, borrowed from Franklin D. Roosevelt, seemed particularly relevant to this post-civil rights generation trying to shed its masks. In this generation, Black executives speak their minds, with doors open. Shawn also does not pause, but rattles off ideas, observations, focused argument and tangents, in a continuous stream-of-consciousness flow.

The consciousness starts. "I'm pro-Black." Shawn says this a lot—over the phone, at restaurants, in casual conversation, and during soapbox sermons. For Shawn, it means thinking Black first. In 1998, he started his own firm, Capital Management Group, a brokerage and asset management house, because he wanted to build Black wealth. When his shop was just getting started he couldn't get a single bank to return his calls. He invested $1.2 million of his own capital to help secure acquisitions so CMG could establish itself. After 5 years, it has already become the ninth largest Black-owned financial institution. In hiring, he goes out of his way to recruit Black brokers—so his staff is not exclusively, but almost entirely, Black. Even the receptionist has a securities license. In business relationships, including hiring vendors—from chauffeurs to office supply companies, Shawn looks for Black first. Even in decorating the Capital Management Group's Chicago offices, he proudly points out that the walls are covered with prints by Jacob Lawrence, not Renoir. It may sound minor but when Shawn was in the corporate world, at American Express and on Wall Street as a trader, he got tired of always being stuck in that classic Spike Lee moment where there were never any brothas on the wall.

So . . .

"I'm pro-Black. I embrace being Black. It doesn't mean that I am anti anyone else but there is a reason we are the lower part of the social economic ladder. We're not stupid or inferior. But there is an exclusionary set of practices right now that occur that stops money from going into our communities. There are all kinds of efforts to take money out of our communities. So I am pro-Black. Uplifting Black people is my number one concern." And the stream ends.

Leadership in the post-civil rights generation has taken some interesting twists and turns. The definition of what it is to be a leader is changing. Expectations are being shaped. Requirements are just being developed. This generation is not looking to a leader, per se, as an elevated, cure-all figure handing down solutions for all problems. For the most part, for this group, leaders are highly individualized, tied to economics, and irreverent, as well as masters of the system. Leaders of yesterday were exceptions and/or extraordinary. This generation is looking for leadership in all of us, every day. They want leaders who are reachable, accountable, and dependable. Leaders are people who can get things done, not people who have been put up on pedestals. It may seem like a jump from Shawn's stream of consciousness to leaders. But, leadership starts with executives like Shawn.

The best example of this is in his shop. Shawn doesn't "let anyone cry victim." When I heard this, I knew that, regardless of his stage cameo, Shawn was very much a post-civil rights baby. More than art choices or hiring patterns, this last part of Shawn's pro-Black mantra is intrinsic to this generation. If you always expect to be hit with something, you learn how to avoid the blows. (Kind of like the Judo metaphor that Wishart of UBS used, which managed to stick even in my sports-challenged brain.) Everyone hosts their own pity party now and then. But this generation refuses to cry victim because they are not interested in explaining themselves to those who don't get it. The only benefit of crying victim is to stir up sympathy. Sympathy, however, doesn't get you very far.

Shawn's office ban on crying victim is not unusual. We've seen it before in the next wave of young Black executives. For this group, this is the heart of pro-Black. Talk to young Black executives and it will seep from their pores. Richard of Booz Allen spoke about the "noise" in the same breath that he concluded that to be successful you have to figure out "how you are going to *deal with that*." Kim at Dell talks of how she has "lost" at the moment her mind moves to victim—"even if I am the victim." You hear this sentiment, phrased in different ways, but still the same sentiment, over and over again. It is embedded in the post-civil rights generation's foundation. Their credentials outpace the height they have reached—that is just the way it is. There are no paths without such stumbling blocks. Instead of stopping, you adapt and move on. So Shawn, like his peers, doesn't let anyone cry victim. "You can get upset about it but you can't complain, the goal is to avoid the mentality of victimization. Take ownership. Life is already random and chaotic," the stream begins to fade again. Then it bounces back for the clincher: "Our problems are our problems whether we created them or not it doesn't make a difference because they're still our problems."

Shawn projects an aura of this attitude, and it made him stand out on that stage. He represented the next generation. It wasn't just his age, which was a decade or so younger then anyone else standing in support mode that day. But, with his highly tailored suit, corporate mannerisms, and pro-Black swagger, he was the perfect example of the new activists—the Brooks Brothas—that this generation produces.

Meanwhile the rest of the people on that stage were straight out of history—a previous generation's solution. It is not Jackson specifically. It could have been Kweisi Mfume of the NAACP, or Marc H. Morial, the new president of the Urban League, or the Rev. Al Sharpton, or the Rev. Calvin Butts. This generation does not fully embrace that concept of leadership—that there is one all-knowing leader with nothing more than a bullhorn and the power of an idea.

To understand just how much the shift away from the old way of doing things is, consider the actions a group of 30-somethings cooked up in California. A few months before Shawn was up on that stage, some of his contemporaries were filing a lawsuit, suing Rev. Jackson for fraud. They call themselves African Americans Against Exploitation Inc., a shadowy group of Los Angeles-based Black men and at least one woman in their mid-30s who seemed to spring up just to file the suit. AAAE Inc.'s lawsuit charged that Jackson "intentionally misrepresented himself as an official of the African American race." The suit went on to ask for a temporary restraining order barring Rev. Jackson from "representing African Americans without their consent."

Let's acknowledge from the start that the lawsuit is unrealistic—a stunt. It is the perfect example of another frivolous suit helping to slow the gears of justice to almost a grinding halt. That said, it didn't stop the shower of Fwd e-mails, with endless levels of snide ha-ha, hee-hee comments tacked on, from cluttering the inboxes of scores of young Black professionals as soon as the news dropped. It struck a chord.

It is the suit's irreverence, humor, symbolism, and gall that is, oh, so this generation. It is a bold public declaration. Instead of staging marches and rallies, this group waged its protest within the structured framework of the system—the legal system at that. It is a perfect example of the Blackprint: taking what you learn from playing by the rules and using it to break the rules. The success of this generation also allows them access to the system. It is no coincidence that the lawyer involved in this case was a 36-year-old Black man and thus squarely a member of the next generation.

The fact that the group would claim to be incorporated also adds to the joke. It is not NAACP Inc., or SNCC Inc., or CORE Inc., but it is African Americans Against Exploitation Inc. This, too, is a nod to this generation's connection to the business world and its need for traditional legitimacy. Even in fun, they think in the language of business.

Then there is the content of the suit itself. The charge, after all, is fraud. Common in corporate and white-collar crimes, fraud usually includes the intent to deceive and intentionally break a contract. In this case, that would be the contract of trust and honest representation. To cite fraud is a blatant challenge of authority within the Black community–generational rift gone public.

"The beef is, first of all, Rev. Jackson has appointed himself leader of the Black community without us getting the ballot to take the vote," says James Stern, 37, the self-proclaimed leader of AAAE Inc. during a shouting match on Bill O'Reilly's conservative playground on Fox News. "Our generation knows nothing about Rev. Jackson. We as the African American community–we're fed up with it."[1]

Not much is known about Stern except that he sporadically pops up on the Los Angeles news scene. In the early 1990s, it was as a minister in Watts brokering peace between Los Angeles gang members and Korean grocers. A decade later, it was as a representative for Black barbers in support of the hit movie *Barbershop,* starring rapper turned actor Ice Cube and comedian Cedric the Entertainer. The 2002 movie was facing criticism and calls for a boycott at the time because of jokes that made fun of the civil rights establishment including Rosa Parks, Martin Luther King Jr., and Jesse Jackson. Besides Stern, the AAAE Inc. also seems a bit shady because its size and members are hard to determine. At different points in its brief moment in the spotlight, news organizations tried to connect the group to Black Republicans and conservatives including prominent Black Jackson critics. But none of the attempts to affiliate stuck.

Most often cited as a culprit behind the suit was outspoken conservative Jesse Lee Peterson, head of BOND, the

Brotherhood Organization of a New Destiny. Peterson has been described as a "self-hating Black man" who "worships at the altar of whiteness."[2] The flamboyant Jackson critic and favorite of conservative news outlets like FOX holds an annual Day of Repudiation of Jesse Jackson, where each year Peterson followers demonstrate outside PUSH offices on Martin Luther King's birthday.[3] Peterson, however, issued his own statement adamantly denying any connection to the lawsuit. [4] Truth is, after filing in Los Angeles Superior court, AAAE Inc. pretty much remained faceless, letting the lawsuit speak for itself; and even with all its frivolousness, it speaks volumes.

Regardless of its shadowy connections, the demand of the AAAE Inc. suit is basically for Rev. Jackson to shut up. It is perhaps the most legitimate way to give someone the finger. No matter how silly the lawsuit is, no one can miss the sentiment it expresses. Most of this generation would never go to the extremes of James Stern and his pals. But it does not necessarily reject the idea that one person cannot speak for all.

As I've said before, this issue of being heard is a big deal. To the post-civil rights generation, allowing a Jackson, or any Black Leader of the Month for that matter, to claim to speak for everyone is inherently offensive. After all, this generation grew up amid the anti-affirmative action inspired "value of the individual" rhetoric. Individuality is now seen as a worthy goal on both sides of the affirmative action debate. It is in the air. What is more significant, this Black generation cherish speaking for themselves. That is why their focus on race is unflinching, even in settings like the office that the groundbreaker generation deems inappropriate. This generation has been doing everything it is supposed to do—from going to the right schools to garnering the right corporate jobs—in hopes that their voices will be heard.

At this point in time, the next generation of Black elite is having trouble being heard and is often just plain swallowed up. On one end, they are drowned out by the noise of the teeming Black underclass, which mass culture uses as the source for all things Black. On the other, they are overshadowed by those who came before—often lumped together as if part of the same breath. But the post-civil rights generation of executives and professionals, bigger than any that came before, with better opportunities and more traditional benchmarks of success gained than any generation to date, is significant in its own right and shouldn't have to share the stage. It simply cannot be assumed that they think the same way and have the same things to say as the generations either before or after (they don't). This group is coming of age now. Their power is just beginning to blossom, which is why it is a good time to listen.

This is where the whole basis of the AAAE Inc. lawsuit really comes from. The complaint that there cannot be an anointed one who speaks for all becomes more relevant when the segment that raises the issue feels that they have never been asked to speak. That is why their suit, as silly as it was, was heard around the world, forwarded and passed along from friend to friend to foe to friend and back again. That is why atop the e-mails, the comments were of the ha-ha, hee-hee ilk. And many people just hit fwd without saying anything; the very existence of the suit, after all, said so much.

So, Shawn, standing alongside the civil rights establishment during that press conference, made an impression. There he was, a young investment banker, head of his own firm (typical post-civil rights credentials), clapping in all the right places, smiling where he had to, and nodding when required. At this point, that is all I knew. "I'm pro-Black" hadn't yet passed from his lips to my ears. Nor had I yet heard his anti-victim crying rule. That would all come soon, but not that moment, that day.

Away from the stage and many pro-Black conversations later, I asked Shawn about leaders, particularly about whether there is such a thing today as a Black leader. Given the setting in which we met, I thought his viewpoint might be particularly revealing. And he did not disappoint: "Shawn, do Black leaders exist today?"

"No! We have to orchestrate our own future because there is not going to be just one person. We need a bunch of leaders who will take a bunch of . . ." Shawn runs out of steam and trails off before finishing the sentence. We both understand that he is talking about taking different directions, paths, ways, or avenues. "Who would do it anyway? Rev. Jackson? His time is done," he says. "Al Sharpton?" he shrugs. "Ken Chenault? He's busy leading his company." After a pause, Shawn concludes, "Everybody wouldn't follow the same person anyway."

It is easy to argue that this generation has no leaders. Yes, there is a hole when it comes to pinpointing up-and-coming Black leaders in the traditional sense. There are no Martins, no Malcolms, no Stokelys, no Angelas, and even no Jesses. The absence of a clear identifiable leader, if that makes any sense, has often been dubbed the next crisis of Black America. Books have been published, discussions have been held, and news articles have been written. In Black circles, "Where is our next leader?" is like asking "What is the meaning of life?" But that misses the point.

Shawn's gut response to my question of whether there is such a thing as a Black leader was, No. He then went on to conclude that even if there was, this generation could never all follow the same person anyway. And *that* is the point. For the post-civil rights generation, one could never speak for all because there is no interest in following. Richard, Alvin, and Susan all wanted to be on top. If there are to be leaders, there must be followers, and that is not what this generation is about. Part of it may be youth, naïveté, and bravado. Even, maybe, a sense of entitlement that is a by-product of new access. Likewise, Black executives double as activists and are leading the movement. It is counterintuitive for business leaders to be followers. Further, the levels of dissatisfaction and frustration that this generation carries are accompanied by a drive not to fall into old traps. What was done before obviously wasn't enough, so they are not interested in repeating it. It is better to try a new approach and fail than to cling to the past. And the past was a Black leader, even Jackson, leading the masses with a dream and a prayer.

Therefore, it is not so much that the next generation does not have any leaders. Instead, because of the isolation, because of the friction, because of the rage, for this generation *everyone* is a leader. Susan jokes about being the ambassador of Black America. But she is. When you are an Only—the only Black VP, the only Black director, the only Black senior manager— the weight and responsibility are undeniably there. But there's a difference. The post-civil rights group has translated that responsibility into leadership. Instead of being overly concerned with the supposed gap in Black leadership, these corporate executives act as if they are all leaders. It is not someone else's problem to solve, but the problem each and every one of us must solve for ourselves.

Remember those Me Too 40-year-olds? They are that contingent of Black-and-proud executives and professionals who wanted to claim the post-civil rights label for themselves. They are probably shaking their heads right now in disapproval over this concept of the individual leaders. Part of that lies in the difficulty any generation has with giving credit to one that follows, like a father who runs his own company successfully for 30 years and then refuses to hear the new ideas that his daughter may have for the family business. Blame it on the nostalgia gene, which wreaks havoc on our memories by spray painting everything with a rosy glow. It then becomes almost against human nature to embrace any departure

142

that the young ones may take. Ever since I tagged him as being too old for my subject sample pool, my friend from the Me Toos likes to tease "my generation." His conclusion is that we are all "a bunch of whiners." As in, What are you writing about "a bunch of whiners"? So my educated guess is that he (and his Me Too cohorts) would not agree that everyone of my generation is a leader. So we disagree.

Every generation would like to think of themselves as leaders in their own right. That is inspiring and helps everyone to move forward. But for the post-civil rights generation, this desire takes on greater meaning since the general consensus is that there is no leadership at large. If there truly is a hole in Black leadership, then each of us in this generation has to become a leader, one by one by one by one.

That is why Shawn constantly tells his staff: "Be the postman. Deliver. In the snow, the thunder, or 100 degree heat, just deliver." The only way for each leader to be valuable is to deliver. What matters is what a person can do or can get done. Idealism, theory, and fiery rhetoric belonged to a past generation; this one is focused on the result. Their definition of leader rests simply on what a person can accomplish.

From this vantage point, it is easy to see why the business world carries such weight for the newest generation of Black elite. Who needs a Black leader when you have Black CEOs? Unlike "Black leaders," Black CEOs control dollars and cents and answer to shareholders, tenements of influence and respect that this nation depends on. That clout can get things done. It makes today's Black business leadership more relevant than rhetoric from a generation ago.

Fundamentally, it is the reason the post-civil rights crowd sees economics as a movement. Black Power Inc. Dick Parsons and Ken Chenault have achieved something that the likes of a Jesse Jackson could only hope for—power within the establishment. That power can be much more convincing than fiery speeches to a generation that walks with raised fists through the best universities and up Fortune 500 ladders. This is a group that has never had to exist outside the establishment. The doors were already open when they were born, remember. They take comfort in knowing that the power of a CEO, even a Black one, is not debatable. It is a power that everyone would acknowledge, regardless of race. This level of respect from mainstream America is unprecedented for Black men. Athletes or entertainers can be held in awe and then explained away as blessed with natural gifts. But, Black CEOs have won at a game in which most Americans deem themselves players. We may not know what it's like to dribble a basketball down center court but most of us know what it is like to try to succeed at the office. Likewise for this bunch, young Black corporate folks, a Black CEO has conquered a world that this next generation is struggling to understand. That matters.

Most important, though, a CEO can accomplish things—like Richard's ideas of using corporate influence and funds for the gain of African Americans. As only a partner at Booz Allen, he felt that he already could do that significantly. Now imagine the impact of the CEO. If this generation is optimistic about anything, it is the assumption that CEOs will want to do something to uplift the race. Or as Shawn says: "The business world builds leaders." Exactly.

That is a clear shift in thinking for Black America. It is this generation's own spin on the situation. Looking for carbon-copy replacements of the civil rights establishment is no longer appropriate or helpful. At its best, the thinking is out of date. It is like searching at a rap concert for jeans that aren't baggy but actually fit. Furthermore, to complain that there are no Black leaders is limiting—the type of thinking that only holds people back. It can be a challenge. I know. I'm a definite glass-half-empty type. The journalist in me, and the post-civil rights baby in me, made sure of that. But it is necessary

144

to move forward. It is the adapt-and-move-on technique that this generation lives by.

There are always doubters. From naysayers who may disagree with the larger significance of Black CEOs to those who question whether progress in the executive suite is truly Black power. When *Newsweek* splashed Ken Chenault, Dick Parsons, and Merrill Lynch CEO Stan O'Neal on its cover as the New Black Power, some Black readers took offense to the headline and the implication that the CEOs could be the next Black leaders.

"The merely serendipitous existence of three Black CEOs of nationally influential corporations no more reflects 'Black power' than the trio of Secretary of State Colin Powell, national-security advisor Condoleezza Rice, and Secretary of Education Rod Paige—or Tiger Woods, Venus Williams, and Marion Jones," writes Chuck Stone, professor at the University of North Carolina Journalism School and a founding member of the National Association of Black Journalists. At the time, Stone was one of only 142 Black chaired university professors in the nation. But he concluded that regardless of his standing at the top of academia, "I do not have a smidgen of 'Black power' to change white racism's ubiquitous persistence in higher education."[5]

The post-civil rights generation has known no other kind of Black power but that of the business world. (Granted, when you are starting from the lowest point, any improvement is great improvement, thus, making the business world the easiest place to see progress.) Still, in politics there are spits and spurts; a Black governor here, a Black Senator there, a few Black congressmen, and some mayors. Even if all were in office at the same time, term limits are a constant reminder of how temporary that power can be. And traditional Black power, in the form of a groundswell social movement is not relevant today. So economics as a movement infuses the outlook of the post-civil rights generation about everything. In one of Shawn's rapid-fire flows, he could express the challenges of Black America only in business terms: "How many of us are going to be CEOs of a Fortune 500 company? How many are going to be CEOs of a Fortune 1000 company? How many of us are going to be SVP at a Fortune 1000 company?" he asked over breakfast before hitting it home, "How many of us are going to jail next year?"

So even if Professor Stone and the rest of the groundbreakers do not believe they have a smidgen of Black power, this generation does. And sometimes, all that is necessary is to believe.

Up until now, we have looked at economics as a movement mostly from the aspect of how that relates to Black leaders. But to confine it to that viewpoint would be an underestimation of power, thus committing the same mistake made by Professor Stone. No one can speak about an economic movement, about business executives as leaders, without also looking at the power of Black consumers. That $688 billion in Black buying power is only getting bigger.[6] The challenge here though is to look at the implications of that number. The value of buying power is influence. Just as corporate executives wield power from the top by the money they control, consumers exert power from their end by the money they control. It sounds simple, but this portion of the equation is not being used to its full potential. What does this really mean? Well, for one thing, it means . . .

"Young Black people affect the world!"

This was another nugget from Oral, the e-commerce executive. Like much of what Oral says, his latest to-the-point bit of wisdom made me think. A month or so after Oral spit this out, there was a small newspaper item: "Campaigns for Black Consumers." It seems that Procter & Gamble, the nation's biggest packaged goods company (look in your cupboards—if you have Tide, Pampers, Bounty, Pringles, Crest, Folgers, or almost 300 other brands, then P&G is in your home), is thinking a lot like Oral.

"We're recognizing that the influence of African American consumers goes beyond the African American market into our general-market consumer," said Susan Mboya, head of P&G's new African American multicultural business development unit.[7] What Black folks buy, particularly what young Black consumers buy, everyone will buy afterward. That is what "Campaigns for Black Consumers" is all about. It is an admission by P&G that mainstream consumers imitate the choices made by young Black buyers. Thus, the company is determined to take advantage of the apparent influence Black folks have on all consumers.

If corporate America can harness that influence, then why can't Black America?

P&G's plan is to bring its Black marketing to the mainstream. Agencies typically develop ad campaigns for Black consumers after creating ads for the general market. So the ad campaign for Crest, for example, is painstakingly developed; then once the slogan and theme have been chosen, an advertising agency carves ads for Black folks, like an afterthought. But P&G has decided to pair its agencies developing ads for Black consumers with its mainstream agencies. For the first time, the Black ad campaign will be part of the general ad development of the brand. P&G is going to increase ad spending to target Black consumers as well as create Black ads for more of its major brands. This means that one of the nation's most influential marketers has openly concluded that Black folks start trends.

Oral is right again: Young Black people do affect the world.

This generation of Black executives understands that they are all leaders. It comes across in their refusal to dismiss race by any means necessary. What they don't get is how empowering that can be. So a bit of whining *is* going on. The situation for Black America is far from perfect; there is always more we can do. But after hearing young Black executives like Sean, Susan, Alvin, Kim, and Bill, to name a few, it is hard to argue that there is no vision or unity. At the very least, there is a definite unity of vision.

But the power that this generation wields lies with each individual. It is the power of paving various paths. It is the power of individual vision with united results. Shawn isn't the only one of this group who is pro-Black. These executives are successful *because* they are pro-Black. It gives them strength; it gives them purpose; it gives them support; it gives them passion to do the impossible.

This generation's new notion of leaders is also important. It affects how they view themselves as Black executives—the power, responsibilities, and significance of that role. In the absence of clear guidance or leadership, left without "the one," Black executives are filling the hole for this generation. That is why there is so much focus about the race, uplift, and doing this for that. We are talking about a highly motivated group, after all. This generation was raised with tales of giants of the past, those who truly changed the world. It is hard to argue with the observation from Alvin, of Sony: How easy it is to look smart when standing on the shoulders of geniuses. Maybe the younger Black professionals just setting foot inside corporate walls for the first time won't feel that pressure. Who knows? But, the post-civil rights group, these 30-somethings, are not yet far enough removed from the groundbreakers to shrug off that pressure and responsibility.

Their success gives them the luxury to concentrate on the intangible issues like the good of the race. What follows, though, is that work then becomes not just a job but a mission. Careers become movements. Whereas, the campuses and churches served as hotbeds for the civil rights era, the Fortune

500 is the breeding ground for the next generation of Black leaders. This generation is driven to succeed because each one of them is a Black leader. *They all have to be.* This affects expectations, tolerance, and relationships. The stakes are high, so expectations are higher and tolerance is lower. In relationships, the higher goals take precedence, so every person is either in the way of those goals or helping. Under such weight, frustration levels can become volatile. And all this is going on in the nation's biggest companies. And that matters, not just to Black folks but to all folks.

So just why was Shawn on that stage? The Shawn who preached that business builds leaders. The Shawn who reluctantly admitted, with the utmost respect and Midwest manners, that Rev. Jackson's time may be done. So why?

"Why not?" he says about his stage post behind Jackson. "We are all strategic tools. Even when your time is done it doesn't make you useless."

Sounds like a leader who understands the Blackprint.

7

WHAT DOES ALL THIS MEAN FOR MAIN STREET?

On behalf of the post-civil rights generation, the Black leader in me would like to thank corporate America.

Thanks for letting us in.

Thanks for making us get all those extra degrees at those great schools before we were let in.

Thanks for always expecting twice as much from us. The quality of what we can do is off the charts now!

Thanks for letting us move up. The slow pace really helped us learn a lot about how you get things done; we feel like we can run things ourselves now, so thanks for the lessons.

Thanks for the glass ceiling—it's a great motivator. We are masters of overcoming obstacles and solving unsolvable problems because of it.

Thanks for paying us no mind. It gave us time to think and develop loads of great ideas.

Thanks for fueling our rage.

Thanks for teaching us how to be entrepreneurs. We are sure you will be doing business with us soon.

And thanks for helping us build Black wealth with those businesses.

Thanks.

Thanks, Fortune 500!

*T*he culmination of the Blackprint and Beyond Rage is that Black executives of this generation are increasingly stepping off the corporate ladder and starting their own businesses. If you think about it, becoming business owners is the logical end point of this ideology. Moving Beyond Rage means avoiding the traps that you already know are out there. What better way to avoid such a trap than by splitting off from the traveled road to create your own path? Sean of BMS is not the only one who's afraid of being pimped. That's this generation's biggest fear—"to wake up and be 45, overqualified, and underemployed, and have to think about how [they] got pimped."

And avoiding that fate is not much to wish for, really.

This new generation is not as patient as the Black executives in power now. Instead, they are emboldened by their credentials and the high expectations that came with that preparation. Don't expect them to inch their way up the corporate ladder by playing yes-men and yes-women for 20 years. If the nation's best companies refuse to award this highly talented new generation of Black executives the positions and power that they deserve, then they will most likely leave the largest corporations to lead smaller ones, leave American companies for foreign ones, or leave corporate America, period, to start their own businesses.

It is the last choice that is most attractive to these pro-Black executives. It is the one that gets the juices flowing. Not everyone is cut out to be an entrepreneur—60 percent of new businesses fail in the first two years.[1] Still, I have not run into a post-civil rights executive yet who hasn't thought about this option, or at least fantasized about it. "I think about it *all* the time," admitted a 32-year-old IT executive on Wall Street who insisted I not use her name precisely for that reason. "Everything else, including the 9 to 5, is just preparing me for that point."

Between 1992 and 1997, Black-owned firms increased 26 percent while businesses overall grew by only 7 percent.[2] In general, African Americans are 50 percent more likely to start a business than whites.[3] That is a huge, definite gap in thinking between the races on an OJ scale. It is a difference that changes outlooks and alters foundations. It means that the exit is an everyday consideration for one group, while for the other, it is more unconventional. For the post-civil rights generation, the dream of building something new is constantly simmering under the surface waiting for the right moment— the day that frustration boils over, or the buyouts are offered, or the side venture is paying enough to be the main gig. The executives at that Black table in the cafeteria are talking about it. They are either thinking about it, have thought about it, or know someone who has stopped thinking about it and is now doing it.

"Our generation recognizes it is a big world. We are not afraid to step out there and take advantage of the choices," says Susan, the ambassador in Colorado, who is in the "has thought about it" stage. "No one wants to stay in corporate America their whole life. If you're lucky you get to leave and run your own thing. That is what really makes a difference [for African

Americans] long term. At least when you're on your own, no one will mistake you for the secretary and ask you to go fetch them some coffee."

Black entrepreneurship is nothing new. Jim Crow took care of that (the *social system,* of course). Corporate America also bleeds talent in cycles. Whenever the economy goes sour or some new craze starts to make people rich (yesterday it was any dot-com; today it's a Krispy Kreme franchise), executives think they can have the good life by running their own show.

There have been ripples of Black flight before, too. In the late 1980s during the days of corporate downsizing, many Black executives walked (or were pushed) out the door, often frustrated with the obstacles of the corporate world. In one of the many dire news stories about the dissatisfaction among Black professionals at the time, the *Washington Post* found a Black midlevel manager who concluded that "corporate America has made a decision to whiten up again."[4] The round of amens could be heard throughout the nation. As a result, there was a blip in Black business start-ups then, too. Some tried their hand as consultants. Others abandoned all semblance of their corporate life, opting to open businesses born of passion. But, many found that the obstacles outside were just as harsh as those inside, so operations remained small and the wave didn't produce any stars.

The difference this time around is that the post-civil rights Black executives have better credentials, experience, and education than those who came before. Black men between 25 and 35 years old with some graduate school experience start businesses more frequently than any other group in the country.[5] More than anyone! In the nation! Think about that. It means the post-civil rights generation is propelling the rise in entrepreneurship for everyone, not just African Americans. These Black professionals also have the Harvard MBAs and have worked inside the nation's biggest and most respected companies. They have performed in a capacity intrinsic to the business of these companies, as opposed to human resources, community affairs, or the EEO posts held by Black managers of the past.[6] This truly is the Black corporate elite.

The latest wave of Black business growth is also not at the neighborhood level of barbershops or family-run funeral homes. Instead, the growth of top-end firms is more than twice as high as it is for Black businesses generally. The new businesses are selling to corporate or government customers; they compete in the broader marketplace. These businesses, often backed by venture capital, are at a level of sophistication that has not been seen before in Black businesses.[7]

Increasingly, highly educated, young Black professionals see starting a business as the natural career trajectory. The goal of the groundbreaking generation was destroying barriers and getting to points previously off limits in the corporate world. But, for this generation, it doesn't matter all that much if the barriers are coming down. There are still plenty of barriers left.

In trying to tell me about my generation, Dick Parsons remembered speaking in the late 1990s before a group of Black lawyers at his old firm Patterson, Belknap, Webb & Tyler. In 1979, Parsons became a partner at the firm. Afterward, he got a call from Conrad Harper, a partner at Simpson, Thatcher. The two had never met before, but Harper wanted to take Parsons to lunch to celebrate. "Now we can start a club," Harper told Parsons. "There are two of us." In 1979, Parsons and Harper were the only Black partners at any major New York law firm. Eighteen or so years later, Parsons stood before the group of young lawyers and listened to them rail about the lack of opportunities. They passionately pleaded their case for better representation. They demanded more Black partners! All things Parsons agreed with. But he also looked out onto the sea of Black faces. At the time, there were about 90 Black partners; not enough, of course, considering there were maybe 4,000 law partners in New York City. But Parsons thought to himself, "It's not a lot, but it is a hell of a lot better than two."

Parsons focused on the tremendous jump from 2 to 90 and smiled. But like that group of young lawyers, I couldn't get past the 90 of 4,000 when he told me this story and frowned. This generation sees the barriers that still exist, and that can be disappointing. So the goal is changing: Instead of plodding along, making incremental changes in the status quo and trying to break down the remaining barriers, they prefer to start fresh and build something new.

It is a trend that is hard to miss. Business professors are talking about it. Small business circles have noticed. Local chamber of commerce groups from Cincinnati (P&G's backyard), to Westchester County (New York's corporate campus central that includes IBM, PepsiCo, and Philip Morris) have seen membership ranks flooded with Black firms headed by young, highly educated CEOs. "The new entrepreneurs are willing to take risks that 10 years ago African Americans were not willing to take," says Barbara B. Lang, head of the Washington, D.C., Chamber of Commerce. "It's an absolute change in attitude, and not having to feel that the corporate structure is the only way—or the safe way."[8]

The trend of Black entrepreneurs with MBAs has widespread implications. Just think how far these new businesses could go. Imagine the possibilities. Think of the industries they could spawn and the competition they could bring. Looking at the 200 biggest companies in the nation, 97 percent have entrepreneurial roots.[9] The stories of Bill Gates, the Harvard dropout behind Microsoft, and Steve Jobs, the computer wunderkind who built a Fortune 500 company from a start in his garage are legendary. But there is also Andy Grove who was barely out of grad school when he started Intel. Jeff Bezos, CEO of Amazon, left his cushy life on Wall Street in favor of the online bookstore that he and his wife had started in their garage. Sam Walton built the Wal-Mart empire on the foundation of one discount store in Rogers, Arkansas. Fred Smith was just 27 years old when he spun a college essay that he wrote at Yale into FedEx. And Arthur Blank and Bernie Marcus are the brains who cooked up Home Depot, splashing everything in the now trademark orange simply because it could be seen from far away and was cheaper than paying for neon signs. Big companies have to start somewhere, and the new wave of Black business owners have the potential to join the ranks of these storied entrepreneurs.

Take Cyveillance Inc. Cyveillance is a technology company that couldn't have existed a decade ago. Born in the dot-com days, it could easily have fallen by the wayside and become just another one of those hard-to-remember names in a field that few understand. But here is a dot-com start-up that actually defines an industry. Using software it developed, Cyveillance helps companies track and protect copyrighted material, trademarks, and other pirated material on the Internet. They are cyber-sleuths. The company scans the Internet looking for counterfeit goods, stolen logos, illegally downloaded movies, basically all the things that make shopping on the Web fun.

Founded in 1997, out of nowhere Cyveillance was suddenly everywhere, gracing the pages of the *Wall Street Journal, BusinessWeek,* the *New York Times,* and *Fortune* as the definitive word on Internet counterfeiting. These weren't puffy dot-com profiles; Cyveillance was instead often cited as the expert in its field. The way Coke knows about soft drinks, or Nike knows about sneakers, Cyveillance knows about cybersquatting and consumer protection. In fact, in 1999 Cyveillance executives were called to provide expert testimony at a Senate Judiciary Committee hearing concerning these very subjects.

Never mentioned in any of this publicity was that Cyveillance was a Black-owned company at the time, started by a couple of post-civil rights executives. In 1999, I had pushed off their PR calls for months because I didn't want to hear about "another dot-com." Then by chance, I saw their CEO Brandy Thomas speak on an Internet crime panel and discovered that Cyveillance was a Black firm. That's interesting, I thought. I still didn't return their PR calls, but I was definitely happy to see that a Black company was being recognized as number one in its field.

In 1997, Brandy, 29, and Christopher Young, 25, were consultants at Mercer Management Consulting in Washington, D.C., when they left their six-figure jobs to start Cyveillance. Chris was a Princeton grad and turned down acceptances to Harvard and Stanford business schools to start Cyveillance. Brandy has four undergraduate degrees from Duke—math, electrical engineering, biomedical engineering, and computer science—and an MBA from Stanford. Brandy's younger brother Jason, 23, was an MIT trained computer geek (MA and BA) who developed the Cyveillance software. A year into business, Chris and Brandy were already raking in hundreds of thousands of dollars from the biggest companies in the nation, including Ford, Bell Atlantic, and Home Depot, all eager for Cyveillance software and consulting services. These post-civil rights executives found a way to force corporate America to come to them.

Cyveillance is still in business and still is considered the definitive voice on Internet piracy. Chris and Brandy (and Jason), however, are no longer there. Back in 1997, they had dreams of making Cyveillance "big," but when the dot-com bubble started to burst in 2000, they did what any smart businessperson should have done—they sold and made a bundle while they could, and moved on (although Brandy admits that

Cyveillance will always be his baby). At last sighting, they were all enjoying the good life their dot-com winnings provided. Chris was thinking about business school again.

The other huge factor motivating post-civil rights executives to start their own businesses is their focus on race. Besides building something big, Chris and Brandy also wanted to "provide opportunity." These pro-Black executives see entrepreneurship as part of their overall goal to uplift the race. The whole Blackprint mentality is based in this goal, and building *that* business is why they are doing any of *this*.

"I am trying to build a legacy, something to pass on to future generations," says Mark Lay, founder and CEO of MDL Capital Management in Pittsburgh. The 11-year-old firm is the largest minority-owned fixed income investment company in the nation. "There are few African American organizations here today that were around 100 years ago and we have to change that. I've been offered millions from larger institutions who want to buy my firm. But, it is not about the money I can make. The goal is for us to build companies that will still be around 100 years from now."

The first time I spoke to Mark, it was two weeks after his 40th birthday. It was a milestone for both of us; it meant that Mark was the oldest of the post-civil rights execs I interviewed. Looking down from that senior post, he had a lot to say. Mark grew up in Aliquippa, Pennsylvania, a poor, rural community about an hour outside Pittsburgh. "I didn't know what a stock or bond was before college," he says, disgusted. He went on to earn a degree in economics at Columbia University. That first year in New York, he interned at Salomon Brothers and did what the business-minded do—fell in love with Wall Street. "There is nothing I enjoy more," he says without a hint of sarcasm. Mark stayed on Wall Street for a decade, first at Citigroup and then at Dean Witter. When he started on the trading floor at Citigroup, he was one of three Black faces out of hundreds of traders. In 1992, at the age of 28, with a wife and two small children to support, Mark gave up his well-compensated job in corporate America and depleted his savings to start his own firm back in Pittsburgh. Starting something Black was *that* important. "My mother was supportive but at the time she really didn't understand why I wanted to leave. In her mind I was better off working at the big firms." Today MDL has $4.5 billion under management and offices in three cities; clients include Boeing and IBM. Michael is a regular commentator on CNBC and his firm's corporate headquarters back in downtown Pittsburgh is housed in what is now known in the city as the MDL building. Never forgetting his Salomon days, Mark's firm has extensive internship and outreach programs with the local high schools in Pittsburgh and, of course, Aliquippa.

This generation is filled with Marks. They are entering corporate America with that—the Blackprint—in mind. The frustration and rage may be what ultimately pushes them to move on, but they go in *expecting* to leave anyway to do something better at some point. This is a common sentiment for young professionals in general, who seldom expect to stay at a particular company forever. And certainly not everyone will make good on their fantasy. But these young Black professionals talk about leaving a system, not just a company, and are doing so because of race. Race is what motivates their decision and triggers their action. They expect to hit an unbreakable ceiling at some point, so they want to learn as much as they can before they hit it and then use their on-the-job education to build their own businesses. Breaking through the ceilings is no longer the point. This is not a full-out dismissal of the established system the way a traditional Black power movement would be. Instead, this generation is doing what it does best: using the system to do whatever they want.

"When you integrate corporate America you learn a whole lot about it," says Shawn, the pro-Black CEO of Capital

Management Group, the asset management firm in Chicago. "I wouldn't be able to do what I do now—run my own financial firm—if I hadn't spent so much time at American Express." Shawn worked there and on Wall Street for a decade before eventually starting his own firm. Today CMG has $1.8 billion in assets under management and seats on the Chicago Stock Exchange.

It is the hidden dream of any marginalized group, any overlooked employee, anyone who has been dumped and dumped on before, to walk out one day and start something better. Even though the post-civil rights generation is using the system as a jumping-off place, it is interesting that they feel the need to jump off at all after the groundbreakers worked so hard to clear a path for them. Kim's crowd-stopping behavior on the stage at Dell during women's history month was striking not only because she was willing to admit in front of the company's CEO that she didn't want to be there more than 5 years, but because she felt passionately that the key to Black empowerment involves more than just succeeding in business; it means *creating* Black business. The strength of those convictions pushes her to be so up front with her exit plans.

This generation's philosophy is not "Business is the answer." It is "*My* business is the answer." That is a big difference. The previous generation focused on proving they were just as good. The best way to do that is to succeed in the established system. Because access had been denied and this had never been done before, the corporate route was ideal for a Dick Parsons or Ken Chenault. But this generation, never having been denied access, doesn't need to prove that they belong. Nor do they feel that they should have to prove they are just as good. They know they belong and are confident that they are as good as or better than their white peers. They have been competing in integrated environments their whole lives, and now the system itself is in question. If Dick Parsons or Ken Chenault had been born a generation later, instead of just running the biggest show in town, they would have expected to start the show, too.

This generation's focus is not proving they are better but that they can *do* something better. The benchmark of success has shifted. This generation, the post-civil rights generation, the generation that has gained the most and gone the farthest wants to use the corporate jobs that integration made possible to build a world that is much closer to the one that existed and flourished before integration.

One of the consequences of civil rights integration was the loss of Black Wall Street. Every city in the United States had one—a thriving Black business community created and fed by segregation. Black families bought food at Black-owned grocery stores, bought their clothes at Black garment shops, got their shoes fixed by Black cobblers, had their health checked by Black doctors, sued each other with the help of Black law firms, lived in houses built by Black contractors, deposited their checks at Black-run banks, had visitors who stayed in Black-owned boardinghouses (not to mention socialized in Black-owned bars and pool halls) and got their hair done at Black salons (okay, some things haven't changed). It was a completely independent Black economy.

The most successful of these Black business districts was in Tulsa, Oklahoma. Its Greenwood section was officially known in Black America as Negro Wall Street. In 1921, the 35-block area boasted 191 Black-owned businesses that created an unprecedented 10 Black millionaires. As many as 600 Black families in Tulsa at the time had assets as high as $500,000.[10] Forget 1921, this type of economic success would be impressive today.

But 1921 would also be the year Tulsa's Negro Wall Street disappeared. Business did not slump, there was no local recession, no economic factor to blame. Instead it was racism. In May, in what became known as the Tulsa Race Riot, thousands of whites stormed Greenwood destroying everything in their path. Hundreds of African Americans were shot, burned alive or tied to cars and dragged to death. The city of Tulsa now admits that it helped fuel the destruction by deputizing a lynch mob. Local leaders at the time, in an effort to quell the unrest, clothed private citizens with the authority to arrest Black residents and thus unofficially with the authority to kill and burn Greenwood. By the time the violence ended, hundreds were dead and Greenwood was completely destroyed. Today, the Greenwood business district consists of a single block.

The post-civil rights generation of Black executives would love to bring Greenwood back. Except in their version, Black Wall Street would serve Main Street, too. It is a hybrid mentality. This generation is not trying to create a completely independent world; they wouldn't need the corporate jobs to do that. They are trying to take the best from both scenarios to create independence without limitations. They want a solid Black business community that everyone would have to buy from. That is the essence of the hybrid approach. The fastest growing Black firms, remember, are the top-end ones that serve the broader marketplace. So they are not thinking of businesses that are small in scope. They are thinking only of businesses that would thrive well beyond those 35 blocks. Businesses, in fact, that would depend on it.

On its face, the hybrid mentality wouldn't seem to mesh with these race conscious, Black, and proud(er) executives of the post-civil rights generation. Why the need to compete in the mainstream world at all? Why shouldn't a completely independent Black economy suffice? Well, for one thing, it wouldn't be good business. Just as corporate America has been jumping on the diversity-of-*dollars* bandwagon—actively chasing consumers in communities long forgotten—Black business is not blind to the larger economic opportunity. This is the most profitable vision. The post-civil rights generation expects to win. This is the best way of winning.

Seeking to build a Black economy within the context of the established business world is also smart. It is a realistic assessment of the world that we actually live in, not the one we would like to live in, and not the one we may be building. One of the biggest stumbling blocks for any new business is an unrealistic view of how things are actually going. It includes the inability of founders to see when it is time for them to move on and let their companies grow without them as well as the inability of larger companies to see that maybe it is time to stop growing so much, so fast. The realistic view of the post-civil rights execs is a sign that the business plan for Black Wall Street is serious. This is not a strategy patterned after the dot-com house of cards, but one firmly grounded in the built-to-last approach.

Lastly, the hybrid mentality truly is pro-Black. It is firmly nestled in the post-civil rights generation's desire to succeed without compromising their Blackness. In the corporate world, they desire to be themselves, to be accepted for who they are, and still succeed. Pro-Black signifies their refusal to ignore race, their refusal to conform to make others more comfortable, and their refusal to deny a single ounce of who they are. Following this logic, therefore, there is no reason Black businesses should not be able to rise to the top of all businesses, competing in the broader marketplace and succeeding despite (or because of) their Blackness. The desire is to build Black companies that are the best at what they do—not just the best for Black folks but the best for all folks. So the goal is always to build a Fortune 500 company. Using the system to change the system is the best way to give the finger to the system that tries to suppress who they are.

I'm reluctant to bring up an example from hip-hop—if only because these days a hip-hop mention is always expected at some point when discussing Black folks—but as far as examples go, it is a good one. For all of hip-hop's "keepin' it real" bravado, it is in essence a hybrid business because the goal is always to be large! To get paid, by any means necessary. That means moving beyond the 'hood. And regardless of hip-hop's foolishness (for a quick peek turn on BET), hip-hop is business. It is one of the nation's leading exports, with sales of more than $5 billion abroad including music, fashion, and movies.[11] Therefore, hip-hop entrepreneurs are businesspeople, and big ones.

And the exemplar? Ideally, it would be Sean Combs if he was not so, well, P. Diddy, but just Sean Combs. Combs has managed to build Bad Boy Entertainment into a $500 million business that includes record sales, artist development, restaurants, a magazine, movies, a fashion label, and 600 employees.

Along with Master P and Jay-Z, he is part of hip-hop's economic triumvirate. All are business powerhouses that have grown beyond the base of music. Of the three, Combs is probably given the least props for his entrepreneurship; making money yes, but entrepreneurship no. When *Black Enterprise* did a series on the hip-hop economy, Jay-Z drew a cover story and Master P much attention, whereas Combs's mentions seemed like afterthoughts.

But Combs has managed to build his empire without a rabid fan base like Master P's No Limit soldiers or a slice of the skills that Jay-Z brings to the art of hip-hop. (Combs also does not have a Damon Dash behind the mic, as Jay-Z does, to build the empire for him.) Instead, Combs has built his empire entirely with his business acumen—lacking die-hard fans and musical talent, that is all he has going for him. He anticipates trends and exploits them masterfully. It is the business, not the art, that he cares about. Bad Boy is stacked with Harvard MBAs. Combs's goal is to grow Bad Boy into a billion-dollar company and then take it public. None of the hip-hop entrepreneurs are thinking on this level. Bad Boy is the closest thing that hip-hop has to corporate America.

Thus, making money, the business, has become part of the definition of hip-hop. The extent to which moneymaking aspirations are openly celebrated in hip-hop is unprecedented in youth culture. While in other parts of society we often feel the need to apologize for making a lot of money and play up altruistic motives, hip-hop artists are respected for their honest acknowledgment that they want to get paid. And the best way to get paid is ruling the business. "I decided to figure out how to do what someone else was going to do with my name and brand anyway," says Combs in *Fortune* magazine, "Not just to make money for myself, but to build a lasting enterprise. I pride myself on being one of the greatest businessmen out there."[12]

While no rap empire today relies only on Black dollars, Combs led the way in the mainstreaming of hip-hop. His product has always been a watered-down pop version of the real thing, inherently intended to attract the widest audience (dollars) possible. His goal has always been to compete outside the world of hip-hop.

The most blatant example of this is his success in the fashion industry. His fashion line, Sean Jean, as opposed to Jay-Z's Roc-A-Wear, Master P's No Limit Gear, Snoop Dogg's Pimp Apparel, and even Phat Farm by Russell Simmons, is not a hip-hop clothing label. He established a high-fashion men's line that favors luxurious suits and formal wear, not baggies and sweats. The line is stacked with designers plucked from other fashion houses; the fashionistas have embraced it and obsessively track its influence. After just 4 years in the fashion business, Combs was nominated by the Council of Fashion Designers of America for men's wear designer of the year alongside Ralph Lauren and Marc Jacobs. (He lost to Jacobs, but that he was even nominated for the fashion's world's Oscar is a sign of the respect that his business has achieved.) With an estimated $450 million in annual sales, Sean Jean is the biggest source of income for Bad Boy Entertainment, the *hip-hop* empire. In 2002, Combs followed the footsteps of Master P and gained total control of his company by buying out Arista records, which had a 50 percent stake in Bad Boy. (Jay-Z's record label, like most rap labels, is a boutique outfit within a larger record company, in this case Def Jam.) I'll spare you a "Benjamin's" cliché, but this latest move does mean that P. Diddy has reached a new level of moneymaking.

In its gut, this generation may respect the independence, focus, and strength of Master P or Jay-Z more than it respects P. Diddy. Master P is the originator of ensuring that every single dollar generated led back to him. By refusing to compromise and insisting on doing things his own way, he retained rights to the masters of his music and gets back virtually 100 percent of the money No Limit earns, partnering with mainstream companies only for distribution. This was a first in an industry infamous for creating wealth for the music labels, managers, producers—everyone except the talent it all started with. That alone makes him a visionary and deserves much respect. (Still, have you seen a No Limit movie? Unfortunately, I have. There should be a do-not-watch warning label on *Da Last Don,* written, directed by, and starring Master P. I wouldn't even want to relive the experience long enough to write about it. So you'll have to trust me; the No Limit empire is not built on quality.)

Jay-Z and Dash have managed to be paid without diluting their product. They have truly created a brand. But Roc A Fella is dependent and tied to Jay-Z. When it works, it's beautiful (think Oprah's Harpo Inc.), but the risks can be devastating (think Martha Stewart Living Omnimedia Inc. after her downfall). What this generation is really trying to achieve is closer to Sean Combs's success, without the Diddy. He is the one who exists within a Black business structure while successfully competing outside. He is the hybrid.

The hybrid approach is relevant because it is also easier for people to grab onto it. Daring, but not too daring. Takes a chance, makes a statement, but is not stupid. That is why the chitchat about the Blackprint, branching off and starting something new, is so pervasive among this generation of Black executives. It is a goal that is not seen as radical at all but fairly commonplace. It is as expected as Working While Black stories or the Twice-as-Hard/Half-as-Far syndrome. Sure, the degrees of the commitment vary. Rhetoric is not always as fiery as Kim's. But these executives are tied together by the greater attention they pay to race, not by their ability to overlook it. So you will probably draw more looks if you're *not* talking about doing something else. The lack of such foresight, even though it might consist of half-baked, unrealistic thoughts instead of concrete plans, could be interpreted as a lack of commitment to the cause. It all goes hand in hand.

"There is a generation of people that are more into pursuing wealth creation now, rather than just saying 'I was dissatisfied because of the glass ceiling,'" says Steven S. Rogers, professor of entrepreneurship at Northwestern University, who studies Black entrepreneurs.

That is Beyond Rage.

For the general business community, the new generation's bold brand of militancy has significant consequences. Black buying power is now $688 billion and counting. A good start, yes. But with the Internet, globalization, and most significantly the business savvy that young Black executives now hold, the economic potential is much greater than any Greenwood.

169

By ignoring the frustration, the rage, corporate America is breeding competition.

Can the Fortune 500 afford a Black exodus? The simple answer is, No. Despite any reservations or concern this generation may have about the corporate commitment to diversity, diversity still holds value. And it is a value that corporate America says it thinks is important. In the most general terms, companies that make diversity and the advancement of its minority executives a priority do better financially. For the past 5 years, *Fortune* has published a list of the 50 Best Companies for Minorities. These are companies where Black executives, and other minorities, hold significant power and presence. For readers, it is often seen as a feel-good list that allows corporate titans a chance to pat each other on the back. But the real news is not who makes the list but that each year the list has outperformed the S&P 500. Even during the rough patches, when stock prices were in the toilet overall, the 50 companies, as a group, did better than average.

Since the diversity case is often short on numerical proof, that is about as good as it gets. Diversity *does* have consequences. The success of Black executives and other minority employees is directly tied to the bottom line. Imagine that. This revelation should outweigh any doubts naysayers may have about the existence of today's Black power.

CEOs know this. When they speak candidly, CEOs acknowledge it was the Texaco case that finally drove this point home. What grabbed the attention of the executive suite was not shocking tapes of offensive language in the boardroom. Nor was it the $115 million payout to settle explosive charges of discrimination. What mattered to senior management was that Texaco's market cap dropped by about half a billion dollars in two days because of the allegations. The stakes are only getting higher. In 2000, a class action discrimination suit at Coca-Cola waged by Black employees forced the company to shell out a record $192.5 million and led to the ouster of Doug Ivestor, its CEO. That is a high price to pay for ignoring the signs.

The rumblings for such an exodus are already happening. It does not mean that come Monday in offices across the Fortune 500 landscape, there suddenly won't be a Black face under 40. Imagine that for a moment, though. No Seans worried about getting pimped. No Alvins with "bullshit" director titles. No Kims to liven up any more panel discussions. No ambassadors named Susan. No Orals to drop verbal nuggets. No Wisharts offering Judo advice. No Ericas on the Street trying to make their mark simply as Black women. No lofty talks with the Richards about impact and noise. No Bills trying to make sense of Blackness. And that would just be a few of the missing. In their place? Nobody, except a whole lot more pro-Black Shawns eager to show off what they've learned and driven to win. A dynamic image isn't it?

Movements don't happen overnight. At least not the successful ones. This generation, however, is starting to come into its own and is about to make its move. At the very least, it must not be overlooked anymore. Because what doesn't happen today, may just happen tomorrow.

The lesson of Greenwood is also clear. The Black economic hub was burned to the ground for a reason. There was tremendous power in those 35 blocks. That was the danger, that was the threat, and that was the problem. The only way to shut down that power was to let it burn, baby, burn. But, there is no reason that a new age of Black economic power, inspired by a Black corporate exodus, could not grow again. Imagine how much more powerful it would be today.

Thanks, corporate America!

8

SEPARATE BUT EQUAL

While I find there's openness and people are very lovely, white and Black, New York is somewhat segregated. And a lot of the separation is by choice. There's a very strong Black society group, with some high-powered businesspeople who come from families to be reckoned with.[1]

—Susan Fales-Hill, socialite and former TV producer

*W*hat is a Black socialite to do? Susan Fales-Hill glanced-over her shoulder teasingly from the newspaper cover spread, her neck wrapped in a vintage Chanel scarf and lobes dripping with diamond tears. Her bare caramel shoulders were draped in an exotic shawl of natural pink roses and fresh flowers that were playfully paired with a luxurious blue ball gown. Fales-Hill, 40, is the daughter of the late Black actress/singer Josephine Premice and Timothy Fales, a white banker's son from Boston old money. The Fales Library at New York University owes its name to her grandfather. The Harvard-educated former sitcom writer and producer, most known for *The Cosby Show* and *A Different World,* spends much of her time these days hobnobbing at various social galas and chairing charity events. She's a socialite in the truest sense.

To say someone has a megawatt smile doesn't mean much in these days of celebrity megawatt everything. But Fales-Hill *does* have a megawatt smile, and it shone from the page. So much so that the headline for the article that went along with her full-page photo read: "Can a Smile Bridge the Divide? A socialite who's a blend of races wonders when the races will blend."[2] Let's try to forget the cutesy, almost offensive, words of the headline. The point of the story was that during Fales-Hill's gilded childhood of the 1970s, guests in her home ranged from Diahann Carroll to Jackie Onassis; today that mix is missing. Socially, there is Black New York and white New York. "At some of the most chic society parties, *especially by the younger set* [emphasis added] . . . a black face is nearly as rare as it was at the Birmingham Country Club in the '50s. And some black philanthropic events . . . aren't little more likely to attract white patrons."[3]

So the socialite, who is married to Aaron Hill, a Black banker and son of a Dartmouth professor, was bemoaning that she had to go to either Black hoity-toity galas or white ones, and rarely anything in between.

For most of us, deciding which gala to go to isn't among our everyday woes. But there is life after work even if it doesn't involve ball gowns. Fales-Hill's observations that younger African Americans were increasingly choosing separate but equal avenues for that life after work is valid—and not just for society folk. The post-civil rights generation is often seeking out Black-only social lives, from the gala to the casual night at home with friends. After 5 o'clock, conceivably, there are members of this generation who do not have any significant relationships or interaction with anyone who isn't Black. They willingly wrap themselves in this *cloak of Blackness*. During one week, a 35-year-old Black media executive went to a Delta Sorority event, a jazz literary tea in Harlem, a Black MBA party, and a long weekend at Sag Harbor, the Black enclave in the Hamptons. The possibility of a full calendar like this isn't happening just one week of the year but most weeks of the year. Even in supposedly integrated venues, this generation has managed to carve out a Black zone. In 1985, Harvard held its first Black alumni weekend, a gathering that was spearheaded by current students at the time—post-civil rights babies. This is no different from the

Black table in the cafeteria. Now the weekend, held every few years, attracts hundreds of alumni, includes a formal dinner and panel discussions, and is sanctioned by the school, even drawing an appearance from the president of the university during the festivities.

It is important to examine how we interact in our private lives because we do not work 24/7, even though it may feel as if we do. Unlike our work existence, our private lives are all about choice and free will. They are the manifestation of our desires and our interests. And in those private lives, this generation often leads a segregated existence. Once the post-civil rights executives leave the office, they retreat back into a comfortable all Black world.

What stands out about the trend is that these Black professionals do not live in a society where such segregation is required. Technically, it is no longer the law. They have the right to go into the whitest section of town and sit down at any lunch counter to eat. Afterward, Mr. Black can take the waitress from that white diner to a country-western bar and they can spend hours shuffling the two-step and drinking Budweisers and end the night hanging . . . out in a coffee shop with friends who never drink coffee. Then Mr. Black and Ms. White can go home to the same building where they can live in apartments across the hall from each other. It could happen, maybe.

Instead, this generation is *choosing* to segregate themselves. This is the action their hearts dictate, and that is a mind-set that doesn't just wash away come 9 A.M. Those feelings, desires, and choices spill into our days at work as well and affect all our interactions, even if subconsciously.

Outside factors contribute to a dual existence of white worlds at work and Black worlds at play. There can be the co-op board that makes things difficult, a mortgage approval that comes in lower than expected, or the rental agency that doesn't return calls. My brother, who is a few years younger than I am and is still surprised by these things, recently called about a house listed for rent in the paper but was told that it wasn't available any more. Ten minutes later, he had a white friend call about the same house, and his buddy was able to make an appointment to see it that afternoon. This wasn't small-town USA a decade ago, but Brooklyn in 2003. Yes, those kinds of real estate games and discrimination are well documented and still with us. So every choice can be steered or shaped by something. "If I get pulled over no one cares if I went to Harvard Business School or if I'm an exec at Sony music," barks Alvin from behind the important-looking desk in his office. "I walk out from these walls I'm just another brother. I consider myself no different. That is how I lead my life. Like just another brother."

Putting aside those outside forces, there is still a huge contingent of post-civil rights babies who are not trying to cross over. They exist in that type of world during the day, and at night they seek the comfort of living, socializing, interacting among their own. Perhaps it is the influence of Black professionals moving back to the inner city as part of an uplift-the-race mission, or simply seeking out Black professional enclaves, organizations, fraternities, alumni groups, cocktail parties, or just chillin'. It is entirely plausible that these Black executives lead a private life that is entirely Black.

When Sean Daughtry and his wife Chenita bought their house in the Roxbury neighborhood of Boston, people in the office couldn't understand it. He is a chemist in Cambridge, and she is a software engineer for IBM. "They were like 'Roxbury!?'" says Sean. "I was like 'Yes—we want to live in the city and we want to be around people who look like us to a certain degree.' You have to be selective to find your own culture."[4]

I thought about my own adult life and had to nod in agreement. After I leave the skyscraper jungle of midtown Manhattan,

I head back to my home in (do or die) Bed-Stuy, Brooklyn. Because my commute is underground in the subway, there is no transition from midtown to Bed-Stuy. The contrast can be striking. Not in a bad way; this is what I choose. My entire adult life has been a game of leapfrog from one Black inner-city neighborhood to the next. By choice. So I, too, am used to the reaction that Sean and Chenita got in their offices when they bought their Roxbury home. It is the reaction that always turns my neighborhood into a question. Bed-Stuy? Harlem? (Before it crossed over.) Washington Heights? Jersey City? Of course, the unspoken follow-up to that question is: Why? Sure, I could afford to live in more integrated areas, but I don't want to. I like to come home to a place and be surrounded by folks who would not think of asking me, why?

The interesting part of this is that there is a good chance that this generation hasn't lived this life before. These are the post-civil rights babies, after all. Although not universal, significant numbers of young Black professionals grew up in integrated neighborhoods and integrated schools, or even predominantly white suburbs and schools. In some cases, they have been the Only their entire lives.

The question then, spoken or unspoken, really is, Why? Why "cloak themselves in Blackness" after living a life that, on the outside, really wasn't.

In one of those bouts when Richard at Booz Allen got serious, he told me about growing up in Park Forest, a suburb 30 miles outside Chicago. One of the first planned communities in the nation, Park Forest, Illinois, was created in 1948 for GIs returning home from World War II. The plan included a downtown commercial district deliberately surrounded by child-friendly curvy streets, front porches, pockets of open spaces, and parks. The design was the first of its kind. The suburb of 23,000 people is conveniently wedged between highways and commuter train stops and less than an hour from major airports. Convenience is the community's prevailing characteristic.

The suburb is also the infamous setting of the classic book *The Organization Man* by William H. Whyte, who defined corporate conformity and warned against its spread in a scathing study of midlevel managers. In his best-selling book, Whyte defined the Organization Man as a "middle-class American who has left home, physically as well as spiritually, to take the vows of organization life. He not only works for the organization; he belongs to it." In exchange for a lifetime of financial security and a "soothing" sense of belonging, Whyte charged, such men were giving themselves to a system that "inhibits individual initiative and imagination and the courage to exercise it against group opinion." Organization men went home to a growing number of new bedroom communities where everyone lived in the same type of house, drove the same type of car, and existed in a world that revolved around children. For the 1956 book, which still influences thoughts on corporate culture today, Whyte interviewed hundreds of faceless managers and their families. The bulk of his research was conducted in Park Forest, Illinois—Richard's hometown.

Despite this characterization as the birthplace of the corporate drone, from its inception Park Forest was one of the few communities in the country established without restrictive covenants. It took about 10 years before the first Black families started trickling into homes on those curvy child-friendly streets. But, early on, the town established a Human Relations Commission to focus on "inter-faith as well as interracial cooperation." By 1958, the Commission and local churches began actively recruiting Black families to move to the community.[5] In the early 1960s, Richard's parents were among the first Black couples to move to Park Forest. "My parents moved to Park Forest because it was integrated," says

Richard almost rolling his eyes the way that teenagers do when referring to the inexplicable decisions of their parents.

The experiment worked; Park Forest is the poster child for integration. Today 47 percent of the village is minority—Black, Latino, and Asian. Richard's schools were integrated. His friends were integrated. Even his church was integrated, and that takes effort, considering 11 o'clock on Sunday is still the most "segregated hour in American life."[6] "It was like growing up in some integrated utopia where everyone prides themselves as such," says Richard. "It was always, 'we are one big happy family' all the time."

This is what the post-civil rights world was supposed to be, wasn't it? Places like Park Forest were supposed to be the reward for a hard-fought war. Get hosed down in the street one day, buy a house in a Park Forest the next. The goal was to be able to live together, learn together, work together, and exist together side by side. At least that is what they taught me in history class. We were all supposed to do what Richard's parents were able to do. Richard's dad was from "dirt poor rural Mississippi" (when Richard says these four words, they are always attached—it is never just Mississippi). Park Forest was a gift for his children; a nice place, a place with good schools, *and* a place where everyone could get along.

However, the ending to Richard's story is that every place he has lived since Park Forest has looked very different. And that has been his choice. Despite his integrated roots, Richard now lives, socializes, and exists outside work in a predominantly Black world. By choice.

His rejection of the we're-all-one-family mentality started when he was picking a college. Choosing between different Ivy League schools, he found himself thinking: "I loved some of them but they reminded me too much of home." Richard settled on the University of Pennsylvania because the campus sat in the Black neighborhood of West Philadelphia. "There

181

was a really strong African American culture there," he said. "That is what I wanted because there wasn't that in Park Forest because it was such an integrated place." That first summer, he came home from school to Park Forest a different man. He overhauled his integrated world into one that was "200 percent Black." "I felt that I had found this missing piece," he says. Richard abandoned the local integrated Protestant church his family still went to and joined one of the biggest Black churches in the area, with a congregation of more than 7,000 members, on the South Side of Chicago.

He also never turned back. True, some of this race-conscious college enthusiasm has softened as he matured—the passions of our youth usually do—but his world outside work is still predominantly a Black one. Most notably, in looking for places to live, he consciously seeks out solid Black communities in contrast to the integrated playland he experienced in Park Forest. As an adult, he moved to New York from Chicago in part because he wanted to take advantage of New York's vibrant Black professional community. He and his wife are raising their four children (a 4-year-old and 6-month-old triplets, yes triplets) in the Black bourgie enclave of New Rochelle. The New York City suburb is home to Ken Chenault, Branford Marsalis, and Earl Graves's son Johnny.

For Richard that is the attraction, that is the point. "In this subset of New Rochelle there are a lot of African Americans doing very, very, very well. So you don't have to deal with a lot of," Richard pauses, "stuff." Richard is talking about the noise again. Richard's choice to consciously seek out something that Park Forest tried so hard not to be is significant because a generation ago, Park Forest was supposed to be the ideal. And that very ideal is what he is rejecting. "For me it is very, very important to be part of a vibrant African American community. Not only for me socially, but for me for whatever difference I can make."

If Richard was the only one, we could brush this off as his issues. But he's not. There are lots of Richards. I'm a Richard. That Roxbury couple are Richards. Here's another Richard: "I don't have to live next to a white family," says Howard Sanders, 32, an investment banker with a Harvard MBA, who gave up his apartment on Central Park West to move to Harlem in the mid-1990s. "I effectively have integrated. I've gone to predominately white schools. I work in a white firm, and I can live anywhere I want. It really is psychologically soothing for me to be in Harlem."[7]

Take a moment to digest the words of this latest Richard. Integration? He's been there, done that. Now it is time to do not what he's supposed to do but what he *wants* to do. And those turn out to be different things. There is no data on the phenomenon but anecdotal evidence strongly suggests that despite the integrated lives of their childhood, the post-civil rights generation likes to keep things Black as adults.

Why?

It shouldn't matter, race, that is. The genetic scientists and biological anthropologists tell us that race doesn't exist. Of the 30,000 to 40,000 genes that make each of us human, only about 6 determine skin color.[8] The *New England Journal of Medicine* concluded several years ago that "race is biologically meaningless." Slice us open and you won't find scientific proof that there are substantial differences between a white man, Black woman, and Asian baby. The DNA is virtually the same. So, yes, it shouldn't matter, this much. But even those who argue that race does not exist biologically, never dare argue that race simply doesn't exist.[9] The reality of our daily lives is that race exists, race matters, race cannot be ignored. Until the academic rhetoric catches up with life, I would much rather use our reality—even if it is a misguided misinformed one—as the starting point. To do anything else is to be overly optimistic, even naive. When race so obviously holds tremendous influence and value in this country, to ignore it is just irresponsible. If we ignore the reality that race exists, we risk ignoring racism and all its ugly manifestations. We know the bogeyman doesn't live in the closet, but when our kids wake up in the middle of the night scared, we do not ignore their cries. Thus, this generation's emphasis on race is just a matter of surviving in the world as we know it.

So why?

Part of the urge for this generation to cloak itself in Blackness directly springs from the integrated settings of their youth. As long as this generation is dissatisfied with the world today, they will want to do things differently. Just as post-civil rights executives don't apologize in the workplace for their Blackness because they remain unconvinced that such behavior helped the generation before, the same holds true for where they choose to live and how they spend their after-hours time. They don't feel any obligation to leave their Black world. In it, young Black corporate VPs from competing Fortune 500 companies mix with Black doctors, lawyers, and chiefs—the kind that head their own businesses. Wall Street egos chat with Black writers and artists and nonprofit save-the-world types. Black academics break bread with pseudointellectuals. This is a world of highly educated, highly successful professionals who are joined together by race. Call them buppies. Call them bourgie. Call them Black. That this social world exists, thrives, and flourishes is a sign that meaningful integration requires much more than just opening a door. Here is an entire generation with such access who still don't feel legitimately welcome.

This Black generation is not the only group that wants to stick together. There are neighborhoods and social networks focused around every group and group subset imaginable. As a society, we constantly surround ourselves with people just like us. Cloaks come in all types including gender, ideology, ethnicity, sexual orientation, religion, specific interest, occupation, income, and, yes, race. So it shouldn't come as a surprise that the post-civil rights generation is doing the same. It is the moniker, "post-civil rights," that gives it more weight. It just doesn't hold the same impact to say, for example, that Generation X is segregating itself. The significance of a Gen X table in the cafeteria is just not immediately obvious. But, when it is the *post-civil rights* generation doing the segregating, it puts things into a historical context that can't be ignored. With post-civil rights, the expectations have been that it would be different. The name says that it should be different. What would be the point, really, if it wasn't different?

The expectations of something *more* are there because this generation occupies a singularly unique place in history. They are the first in this brave new world, like the children of war survivors, and as the children, they are without the weight of the memory of the way things were. This generation has never known a world where, at least legally, the door was not open. That is why their expectations can be so high. So the past can seem (artificially) very long ago. Their actions are the first indication of the war's legacy, so the choices they make are not like those of any group that came before.

Without the burden of memory, it is easy for this generation to lose perspective, which is not necessarily a bad thing. Such naïveté allows them to take roads that they truly want to take, because they haven't learned yet what they are supposed to do (or can't do). It is similar to a first love, when feelings are honest and open and always on the surface because we haven't yet learned to hide such things. The breakup of that relationship can be crushing. So the next time around, we keep a little bit back so it won't hurt so much when it's over. This generation is having Black folks' first relationship after the civil rights movement. That is why their actions are significant. They are honest and open and everything is on the surface because they haven't learned yet what to hide. True, youth gives us all the benefit of this honeymoon just once. But not everyone's honeymoon happens at such a pivotal moment in history. Only *one* generation could be the first to be born and raised after the civil rights movement. This is it.

That said, what remains is that this generation is not convinced Park Forest works. We are a nation of different boxes stacked on top of one another. Maybe an integrated utopia is not the answer. Even if it is, until all types of people get the respect that they deserve, it can't work. So maybe it is not the answer, yet. "You can say Park Forest is a microcosm of the world or you could say it is something very different from the rest of the world. I would say it is very different," says Richard.

That is telling. Integration cannot work if those who are truly experiencing it (a sprinkling of tokens was not the goal either) constantly feel as if their world is the exception. That result is not a societal change but a lab experiment. Often we dwell on how much things have changed. And, thankfully, yes they have. But by not recognizing how much things have *not* changed, we run the risk of slipping backward. When you think you are very far ahead in a race, it is natural to relax, just a little, because you're winning and there's no need to use up all your strength. When the lead is narrower, you don't have that luxury if you still want to win the race. This generation refuses to relax. So Richard, a product of a planned integrated community, doesn't believe that he grew up in the real world. More significant is that, instead of seeking another exception like Park Forest, he rejects the idea altogether, finding comfort under the cloak of Blackness.

This mirrors what is going on in the office. This generation does not expect a 9-to-5 without the frustration or the noise—that is the basis of Beyond Rage. They don't even expect to find a Park Forest exception when it comes to the workplace. Such lack of surprise is no different from rejecting the exceptions. In both cases, the situation—the state of race relations—is seen as a constant that will not change. Instead of trying to change the situation, this generation adapts to it.

Is the post-civil rights generation losing something by lowering its expectations when it comes to integration, or as the *New York Times* asks, when the "races blend"? Just as race is a reality, it is also a reality that Black folks live in a multiracial society. As part of that society at large, it can be worrisome if we constantly accept being relegated to enclaves. So is this generation cheating itself by not taking advantage of all the possibilities? I don't think I'd go that far. To do so would be to completely devalue the "cloak of Blackness." To be cheated would mean that the cloak is somehow not as good; that a Black gala that Fales-Hill might choose to attend is not as prestigious as a white one. So I wouldn't say cheated.

One of the reasons Richard chose Booz Allen versus other consultant firms is that he "wasn't going to have to be a trailblazer." Booz already had Black partners. Richard and much of his generation aren't looking to be trailblazers—access was yesterday's battle, today it should already be here. Instead, Richard and this generation are more concerned with what they can do now that they are allowed through the door. What they are discovering is that access is meaningless if barriers have not really been broken down but merely repositioned. The remaining rubble can be just as difficult to climb over. What does it matter if we can live anywhere we want, go anywhere, work anywhere, play anywhere, if we still aren't comfortable or accepted once we get there? As a result, this generation is forgetting that just gaining access also has value. It will always have value to some extent. So maybe we shouldn't be so eager to give it up.

The implications of the segregated choices that this generation is making reach far. Most significantly, they affect how our future children will be raised. The children of this generation on both sides will know only segregated worlds and not by choice. Think about the school system, for example. Many of our classrooms are already separate. Today, one out of every six Black students in this nation attends a school that is almost 100 percent nonwhite.[10] Now what if that number was much higher? And no one ever suggested it should be different. By removing themselves, this generation is not only making a choice for themselves but for those, Black and white, who will follow.

This is not to say that there is nothing to gain from the cloak of Blackness. The most basic payoff is peace of mind. Richard thinks big thoughts about everything; it affects how he works, how he lives, and every decision in between. It is the weight that all share who are concerned about, simply, the state of Black folks. Period. This generation of Black professionals doesn't have to choose to care, but sometimes it can be just as much work to act as if they don't. After a day of carrying that weight, Richard doesn't want to come home and deal with more stuff or noise. Those moments of letting go are precious. (They are also taken for granted by the mainstream.) But, carving out space where you feel entirely comfortable is part of survival. If that happens under the cloak, then so be it. It is how we rebuild our strength and restore our confidence. Such value cannot be overlooked. No one can fight every hour of every day. Peace of mind is necessary to move forward.

The other payoff is power. And a payoff that big is worth anything that may be lost along the way. The problem with integrated fantasies is that success is dependent on dividing communities. To be truly integrated in work, play, and life, no group can dominate, everyone should be on equal footing. That is fine, a beautiful thing if it happens, and would probably create a society where everyone has the possibility to reach his or her full potential. I would imagine it would be the healthiest world in which to live. But it may also be an impossible dream. If not, then at the least, today's reality is something different.

So, there is no sense throwing away the strength of unity. Not to sound like a Hollywood football locker room pep talk, but this generation is trying to hold on to the strength that comes from being part of a team. A population trying to grab power cannot afford to be divided. By living together and socializing together, this generation sheds the status of Onlys and becomes a force, even if for just a few hours a day. Not only does this type of community breed ideas, relationships, and energy that can make things happen but it reminds the members that they are indeed not alone, which is empowering. That kind of support is invaluable. So, go team!

Thinking back to one of the Richards—in this case, Howard, the investment banker in Harlem—the mere act of reaching for the cloak of Blackness can be powerful. There is strength in the assertiveness of his words: "I don't have to live next to a white family." This generation is willfully going against what is expected and making decisions for themselves. It is part of their ongoing challenge of the meaning of success and part of their continuous quest to succeed without compromises. Howard declares: "I can live anywhere I want." And then he *chooses* Harlem. This is action, taking charge of the situation and making a statement. He is enforcing his choice. This generation can live anywhere they want, go to any gala they want, chill with anyone they want, and what they want is Black. That inherently raises the value of Blackness. It is simple economics. The more someone wants something, the more valuable it becomes. Diamonds are valuable because as a society we have made those compressed chunks of coal desirable. Sure, supply issues are involved; diamonds are the least common form of coal and so that adds value. But, hummingbirds aren't too common either, and they don't have the value of diamonds. So it is not just the supply but *demand*. As a society, we have said that one form of coal is more valuable than another form of coal. Likewise, because this generation is demanding the cloak of Blackness, its inherent value is rising. It is saying that the cloak is valuable, not something that this generation is settling for or even just accepting. The cloak is their first choice. Instead of fighting to get out from within it, this generation is fighting to stay in its warmth because it is worth that much and is that valuable.

Understandably, the concept of reaping power by rejecting integration may sound startling. It goes against everything we've been taught and is contrary to inherent hopes and beliefs. It is also dangerous to advocate something that can so easily be twisted, exploited, or misunderstood. But, there is a definite difference between choosing a segregated existence and being trapped or forced into one. With choice comes control. That is power. People living under a dictatorship have the least amount of power because they have no choice. Choice also includes will. Power again. Choice broadens possibilities instead of limiting them. Powerful. All that power comes when choosing the cloak of Blackness.

The challenge for my generation will be to realize the power of our choices, to make those choices wisely and to the fullest extent, and then take advantage of all the purpose and influence that choice can wield.

The point of all this is that something isn't working. Perhaps this generation is a bit impatient as Dick Parsons and the groundbreakers suggest. I don't agree. But, if so, better impatient than complacent, so I take it as a good sign. Besides, any impatience still doesn't change that we are not "there" yet, which means all sides are losing out. Sure the cloak is powerful. Ideally, though, a mix is always better than colonies of separates. That is how society is challenged, grows, and improves; but it only works if it is a mix of equals—otherwise, it isn't a mix at all but a takeover. And I'd rather stay independent.

We have been taught that separate but equal is impossible. What about separate but better? Is that impossible, too? For a generation of hybrids, what really constitutes separate, anyway? This generation is experimenting and playing with these boundaries. Instead of a hard-and-fast line, it dips and rises continuously and the result is unpredictable.

These are the things I thought about that Sunday when I saw Susan Fales-Hill and her megawatt smile, the one that prompted reporters to "wonder when the races will blend." This is why I wasn't surprised when I learned about Richard's Park Forest past versus how he chooses to live now. This is what I think about on my subway ride from midtown to Brooklyn. Some think these choices are a step backward, and others suggest they might be suffocating. But I'm comfortable with such choices. During the day, I'm reminded that there are things much more suffocating. That is why I like coming up for air in (do or die) Bed-Stuy.

AT LAST

The end?
—Cora Daniels, author, *Black Power Inc.*

*T*his is not a Conclusion! A conclusion would mean that the conversation is over. Conclusions have no place in books that want to further discussion. It is not an Afterword or an Epilogue; they both sound kind of dispensable and imply that you've come to the end and it's time to sum up. For me, they've always meant the extra chapter at the end that is not really necessary. The temptation, then, to read every three words instead of reading every other word is just too great. In high school, I had a bad habit of never reading a single page beyond the last chapter. Nothing titled Afterword, Epilogue, and certainly not Conclusion, would I read. There was no need to rehash everything I had just read. So, instead, let's say these final pages are Last Thoughts . . . for Now.

What's the point? Why did I bring you through this journey? Why did you take it?

The point is, this generation has something to say. Race is more important, not less. Period. This is not a handicap or a burden either. It is an honest assessment. And it is power. Armed with that truth, this generation is doing things differently. Period.

This generation is aggressive, focused, impatient, unwavering, bold, and demanding when it comes to race. Black is first; Black is what matters; Black is important. They have managed to turn mainstream success into a kind of militancy that doesn't reject the system but uses the system for its own goals. That is new. That is powerful because the results should be longer lasting.

Coincidentally, one day splashed across the front page of the *New York Times,* the nation's paper of record, was a story about young African Americans and the Democratic party. The article discussed politics specifically, but it was really about so much more. It was a good illustration of how this generation thinks in general. Apparently the Democratic party is "perilously out of touch with a large swath of Black voters—those 18 to 35 years old who grew up after the groundbreaking years of the civil rights movement."[1] Whereas Democrats have traditionally counted on more than 90 percent of the Black vote, such loyalty is not guaranteed among young Black voters. Sixty-three percent of Black voters in 2003 considered themselves Democrats (down from 74 percent in 2000). But among Black voters under the age of 35—the post-civil rights babies— almost 35 percent now consider themselves Independents versus 24 percent of Black adults in general. This is doing things differently. One political pundit concluded: "This group really should be considered swing voters to be targeted specifically. But if you look at or listen to the typical political ads aimed at black voters, there is a huge disconnect with younger African Americans." Duh! Indeed, there is a shift, and it is not just in politics, but in all aspects in life *and* work.

The content of the news story is not surprising. Of course, the post-civil rights generation of African Americans does not think like the generation before. The fact that this was front-page news is what surprised me. It was news because no one had asked my generation what we thought before.

According to this front page news, polls show that compared with their parents and older African Americans, these younger African Americans place a higher priority on issues like racial profiling and protecting civil liberties. Think about it. That's race stuff, really. In the 2002 governor's election in Maryland, it was young Black voters, focused on race, who helped elect the first Republican to the statehouse in 36 years. The Republican ticket included a Black running mate, Michael S. Steele, for lieutenant governor. Steele's team created special ads specifically for hip-hop radio stations—the perfect outlet to reach the post-civil rights generation. Trying to tap into frustration among these Black voters over the Democrats' all-white slate, the radio spots used tag lines like "Why must African Americans always wait?" It hit a nerve. The Republican ticket ended up capturing 14 percent of the Black vote, the largest percentage of Black votes ever for Republican candidates in Maryland. In Baltimore, which was flooded with the hip-hop ads, the ticket received 30 percent of the Black vote, fueled by the post-civil rights generation, which turned out in force. This is doing things differently, too, much like the way this generation navigates the business world. No matter what the venue, this generation is determined to do things their own way. And that's the point.

"I believe African Americans have no permanent friends and no permanent enemies, only permanent interests,"[2] says Sylvester Smith, 27. Smith wasn't talking about the Maryland race, but he could have been. He wasn't talking about his own situation either, but he could have been. (Smith is the policy advisor on Minority Affairs for the Republican governor of Arkansas. His mother was a Democratic state legislator.) Instead, he was just talking. After the many months I spent talking to the post-civil rights generation—my generation—it occurred to me that he could have been talking for us all.

The point is, Beyond Rage is a movement for this generation. And we are all leaders.

When I first spoke to Sean, the marketing exec at Bristol-Myers Squibb who uttered the pimped line, he was 32 days away from a make-or-break product launch and an expected 34 days from becoming a father. He had to make a choice: lead the product launch meeting that was supposedly necessary for a promotion he thought was long overdue, or participate in the birth of his first child.

The day of the meeting, Sean's son was born. As a storyteller, I appreciated the timing. Sean never got on the plane for the meeting that he had worked for months to put together. He chose to be by his wife's side instead welcoming his son into the world. By all accounts, though, the three-day meeting in Palm Springs was a hit. The rave reviews were still flooding in when we caught up a month afterward. People were generally wowed by the substance and presentation. Sean's post-civil rights membership was also very much felt. Queen Latifah served as a celebrity host for the BMS crowd. The spoken-word artists of *Def Poetry Jam,* the Russell Simmons Broadway show, provided entertainment for the pharmaceutical executives. Two weeks after the meeting, the HIV drug that Sean had done all this work for (this was a product launch meeting, remember) received FDA approval. For a marketer, it was like the icing.

Sean also got his promotion. Not with BMS though. His promotion came via Pfizer, its biggest competitor. The launch meeting was supposed to be Sean's last hoop to jump through. The promotion that he had been told time and time again was coming, would come, *after* the meeting. But when everyone got back from Palm Springs and Latifah's bling bling lost its shine, the "it's coming" talk started up again instead of "it's here." So he left. The last time I spoke to Sean, he was to start at Pfizer in a few days. There, as a team leader, the marketing executive would run the pharmaceutical company's entire HIV business. It is a significant jump from his role at BMS. Sean will also be the only Black team leader in the entire marketing operation at Pfizer. "The dynamics will be interesting," he laughs nervously.

That is Beyond Rage in action. It is a company product launch meeting highlighted by hip-hop poets. It is not waiting for "it's here." It is the expectation of "dynamics" that will come from being the only Black face at his rung on the ladder. It is no different from the election in Maryland. Sean refused to compromise an ounce of who he was and found a way to succeed anyway.

When I was talking with Ken Chenault and he was saying things that someone from his generation wasn't supposed to be saying, he threw out a tidbit of advice that has stuck with me. It was about the opportunity of uncertainty. Chenault believes that for Black executives, uncertainty is the best opportunity. "When there is substantial change and uncertainty, people look at original ideas, alternative leadership techniques, and are more open to accepting a nontraditional person in a major role. If things are going well, people are less likely to take chances."

If that is true, the time for this generation has come. We now live in uncertain times, from the downward spiraling economy to the global unrest and upheaval, to the local political unpredictability. It is like a perfect recipe for the "change and uncertainty" that Chenault mentioned. And this generation is indeed fighting—for the whole pie. This generation is finding ways to succeed in all aspects of life without compromises.

That can be tough. No, it can be harder than tough. It can seem impossible. The most common thing folks would ask me about during all those conversations was whether they were the only ones. Is it just me? No, I'd say, then think of Sean. We are all trying not to get pimped.

What are you? The sooner you figure that out, the sooner you will succeed. Over dinner, Derrick, a 34-year-old finance executive, started talking about his firm's Black employee group and his observation about those Black executives who try to shun the group. "They don't do as well," he says, as matter-of-factly as "pass the salt." In his mind, one never needs to apologize for Blackness.

Derrick wasn't talking just about the group in his company but The Group, in general—the Black table in the cafeteria, the Black professional networks, the Black social ties, The Group. There was no way I could disagree with his pass-the-salt conclusion. Even if those who shun The Group start out moving faster than the rest of us, for the most part, they can't survive. At some point, they will need someone to hold on to. Back in the third grade, the kids with the bowl haircuts made sure I learned that race divides and unites. And always matters. Who are the *raceless wonders* going to hold on to when that point comes? Race is not a burden. It is an essential part of who we are, and to ignore it is like trying to walk with one leg or maneuver without thumbs. To deny race is to live a lie, which limits potential. It is cutting off a thumb.

In anything we do, there is always an "Ah-Ha" moment when it all makes sense. It doesn't necessarily have to be a "big idea" explosion. Sometimes it could just be hearing our deepest thoughts come out of someone else's mouth. For me, that's what happened when Sean, then at BMS, uttered his infamous words: "I don't want to wake up and be 45, overqualified, and underemployed, and have to think about how I got pimped." That is why I started these conversations, to find those voices and let them be heard. That one line could not and cannot be forgotten. That voice is being heard, and more like it will be heard. The conversation is not over; it's really just beginning.

We are the post-civil rights generation. We are young, Black, and proud. That is the point. And that combination presents endless possibilities. Youth is what energizes us, pride is what drives us, and Black is what supports us. This is a generation of Black executives first, not executives who happen to be Black.

What am I?

My answer is still the same. It is just the question that follows that is slightly different. I am a Black woman. Before I asked, now what? This time I ask, what now?

So . . .

What am I? I am a Black woman. What Now?

Notes

Chapter 1: Working While Black

1. *The Reality of Intentional Job Discrimination in Metropolitan America–1999,* Study was commissioned by the EEOC and conducted by Alfred W. and Ruth G. Blumrosen of Rutgers University. Results were released in 2002.
2. David A. Harris, *Driving While Black Racial Profiling on Our Nation's Highways,* University of Toledo College of Law, An American Civil Liberties Union Special Report, June 1999.
3. David W. Rasmussen and Bruce L. Benson, *The Economic Anatomy of a Drug War: Criminal Justice in the Commons,* London: Rowman & Littlefield, 1994.
4. U.S. Department of Justice, Local Police Departments, 1997, and Sheriffs' Departments, 1997, Bureau of Justice Statistics. This is a division within the Department of Justice that puts out research papers. Andrew L. Goldberg and Brian A. Reaves are BJS statisticians who did both reports. Number is sum of numbers from both reports (released February 2000).
5. Gene Callahan and William Anderson, "Roots of Racial Profiling," *REASON,* August/September 2001. Information was also gathered from Schaffer Library of Drug Policy.
6. Erica Frankenberg, Chingmei Lee, and Gary Orfiled, "A Multiracial Society with Segregated Schools: Are We Losing the Dream?" Civil Rights Project, Harvard University, Jananuary 2003.
7. Ron Stodghill and Amanda Bower, "Where Everyone's a Minority: Welcome to Sacramento, America's Most Integrated City," *Time,* September 2, 2002, p. 26.
8. In 2000, Coca-Cola settled the largest racial discrimination suit ever for $192.5 million. Texaco settled its high-profile racial discrimination suit in 1996 for $176 million.
9. Marsha Low, "From White to Black: Once an Integration Model, Southfield Sees Population Shift," *Detroit Free Press,* June 6, 2001, p. A1.
10. See note 1.

Chapter 2: Beyond Rage

1. Ellis Cose, Ch. 1: "Why Successful People Cry the Blues," in *The Rage of a Privileged Class,* New York: HarperCollins, 1994.
2. "What African Americans Think of Corporate America," Joint Center of Politics and Economics exclusive survey commissioned for *Fortune,* June 6, 1998, p. 140.

3. Patricia Brown, "The Broken Ladder", *Consulting Magazine,* July 2002, pp. 18–24.
4. See note 2.
5. Roy S. Johnson, "There Is Opportunity and There Is Action," A conversation with Hugh Price of the National Urban League, *Fortune,* August 4, 1997, p. 67.
6. See note 1.
7. See note 5.

Chapter 3: Sistas Unite! Are Black Women Corporate America's Forgotten Threat?

1. U.S. Bureau of Labor Statistics.
2. National Committee on Pay Equity.
3. *Working Mother* magazine survey, "Best Companies for Women of Color," June/July 2003 issue.
4. "Flurry of Hate Crimes Shocks Denver," *Associated Press,* November 22, 1997. Also local coverage in the *Denver Post* and Denver *Rocky Mountain News.*
5. Ella L. J. Edmondson Bell and Stella M. Nkomo, *Our Separate Ways: Black and White Women and the Struggle for Professional Identity,* Harvard Business School Publishing, 2001.
6. *Cellblocks or Classroom? The Funding of Higher Education and Corrections and Its Impact on African American Men,* a report released by the Justice Policy Institute, 2002.
7. U.S. Department of Justice's Bureau of Justice Statistics Bulletin "Prisoners in 2000," Allen J. Beck and Paige M. Harrison, BJS statisticians.
8. *Journal of Blacks in Higher Education.* Vital Statistics Bulletin.
9. Ellis Cose with Allison Samuels, "The Black Gender Gap," *Newsweek,* March 3, 2003, p. 46.
10. *Women Business Owners of Color: New Accomplishments,* Center for Women's Business Research, Continuing Challenges 2003 Report.

Chapter 4: Dissed by Diversity: How Diversity Became a Dirty Word

1. Linda Greenhouse, "Justices Back Affirmative Action by 5 to 4," *New York Times,* June 24, 2003, p. A1.
2. Linda Greenhouse, "Context and the Court," *New York Times,* June 25, 2003, p. A1.
3. Nicholas Lemann, "Beyond Bakke: A Decision That Universities Can Relate To," *New York Times,* June 29, 2003, Week in Review Section 4, p. 14.

4. Neil A. Lewis, "Some on the Right See a Challenge," *New York Times,* June 24, 2003, p. A1.
5. Steven Greenhouse and Jonathan D. Glater, "Companies See Law School Ruling as a Way to Help Keep the Diversity Pipeline Open," *New York Times,* June 24, 2003, p. A25.
6. Robert J. Grossman, "Are Diversity Programs Truly Effective?" *Wall Street Journal, Career Journal* (it is a special online section for subscribers), March 2000.
7. Delyte D. Frost, "Review Worst Diversity Practices to Learn from Others' Mistakes," *HR Focus,* April 1, 1999.
8. Cultural Diversity at Work.
9. Fay Hansen, "Diversity's Business Case: Doesn't Add Up," *Workforce,* April 1, 2003, p. 28.
10. U.S. Census Bureau. National Population Projections: Projections of the Resident Population by Race, Hispanic Origin, and Nativity 2050–2070. These projections were released with the 2000 census.
11. *Business Case for Diversity,* Diversity Inc., 2003, p. 1.
12. Follow up *Workforce 2000* study by the Hudson Institute, 1990.
13. David Gates, "White Male Paranoia," *Newsweek,* March 29, 1993, p. 48.
14. Michele Galen, "White, Male, and Worried," *BusinessWeek,* January 31, 1994, p. 50.
15. Jacqueline A. Gilbert and John M. Ivancevich, "Valuing Diversity: A Tale of Two Organizations," *Academy of Management Executive,* February 1, 2000, pp. 93–105.
16. Robert J. Grossman, "Should You Seek a Strong Diversity Program?," *Wall Street Journal. Career Journal,* February 2001.
17. Jeffrey M. Humphreys, "Multicultural Economy 2003: America's Minority Buying Power," Selig Center for Economic Growth at the University of Georgia.
18. Gail Robinson and Kathleen Dechant, "Building a Business Case for Diversity," *Academy of Management Executive,* August 1, 1997, p. 21.
19. Dan Barry, David Barstow, Johnathan D. Glater, Adam Liptak, and Jacques Steinberg, "Correcting the Record: *Times* Reporter Who Resigned Leaves Long Trail of Deception," *New York Times,* May 11, 2003, p. A1.
20. Lynne Duke and Darryl Fears, "Putting Diversity in the Line of Firing: Minority Staffers at the *Times* Feel the Loss and Fear the Fallout," *Washington Post,* June 7, 2003 p. C1.
21. David Leonhardt, "Losers All: 'Egalitarian Recession' Keeps Anger at Bay," *New York Times,* June 15, 2003, Week in Review Section 4, p. 1.
22. Fay Hansen, "Diversity's Business Case: Doesn't Add Up," *Workforce,* April 1, 2003, p. 28.
23. "Knight Ridder in Cost Cutting Scavenger Hunt," *Dow Jones Newswire,* February 10, 2003.

Chapter 5: Generational Warfare

1. Lonnae O'Neal Parker and Darryl Fears, "Boyd: Race Was No Factor with Blair," *Washington Post,* August 8, 2003, p. C7.
2. Johnnie L. Roberts, "The Race to the Top," *Newsweek,* January 28, 2002, p. 44.
3. See note 2.
4. Nelson D. Schwartz, "What's in the Card for Amex? New CEO Ken Chenault Has No Shortage of Plans for American Express," *Fortune,* January 22, 2001, p. 58.

Chapter 6: This Generation Needs No Leaders

1. "The O'Reilly Factor," *Fox News,* November 20, 2002.
2. Michael Eric Dyson, "Self-Hate beyond Debate," *Chicago Sun-Times,* August 6, 2002, Editorial, p. 27.
3. "*San Francisco Examiner* African Americans versus Jesse," *CNN,* November 20, 2002, and *Associated Press,* November 22, 2002.
4. BOND Press Release, November 22, 2002.
5. Chuck Stone, "Letters for New Black Power Issue," *Newsweek,* February 11, 2002.
6. Selig Center for Economic Growth at the University of Georgia estimated that Black buying power was $688 in 2002. By 2008 it estimates Black buying power to reach $921 billion.
7. Stuart Elliot, "Campaigns for Black Consumers," *New York Times,* June 13, 2003, p. C5.

Chapter 7: What Does All This Mean for Main Street?

1. Brian Headd, "Redefining Business Success: Distinguishing Between Closure and Failure," Small Business Association, Office of Advocacy, March 20, 2002.
2. U.S. Census Bureau, 1997 Economic Census data.
3. *The Entrepreneur Next Door,* 2002 Panel Study of Entrepreneurial Dynamics, Ewing Marion Kauffman Foundation, September 2002.
4. Dorothy Gilliam, "Corporate Career Crisis," *Washington Post,* January 8, 1987, p. D3.
5. See note 3.
6. Sharon Collins-Lowry, *Black Corporate Executives: The Making and Breaking of a Black Middle Class,* Philadelphia, PA: Temple University Press, 1996.
7. Timothy Bates (Wayne State University) and William D. Bradford (University of Washington), *Minorities and Venture Capital: A New Wave in American Business,* Ewing Marion Kauffman Foundation, July 2003.

8. Daniel Altman, "Young African Americans Try Entrepreneurship," *New York Times,* May 6, 2003, p. G8.
9. See note 5.
10. Gregory S. Bell, *In the Black: A History of African Americans on Wall Street,* New York: John Wiley & Sons, 2002.
11. Alan Hughes, "Hip Hop Economy," *Black Enterprise,* May 2002, p. 70–75.
12. Nicholas Stein, "Celebrity Inc.," *Fortune,* September 17, 2001, p. 164.

Chapter 8: Separate but Equal

1. Cathy Horyn, "Can a Smile Bridge the Divide?" *New York Times,* April 27, 2003, Section 9, Styles, p. 1.
2. See note 1.
3. See note 1.
4. Johnny Diaz, "Now the Gentrifiers Are Black," *Boston Globe,* September 15, 2002, City Weekly Section–Roxbury, p. 1.
5. Larry McClellan, "Park Forest," *The Star,* February 24, 2002, p. A5.
6. Martin Luther King Jr. from his sermon "Paul's Letter to American Christians" given at Dexter Ave. Baptist Church, Montgomery, Alabama, November 4, 1956. He also used the quote in his first book *Stride Toward Freedom: Story of the Montgomery Bus Boycott,* New York: Harper & Row, 1958.
7. Lisa W. Foderaro, "For Affluent African Americans, Harlem's Pull Is Strong," *New York Times,* September 18, 1998, p. A1.
8. Dr. Joseph L. Graves Jr., *The Emperor's New Clothes: Biological Theories of Race at the Millennium,* New Brunswick, NJ: Rutgers University Press, 2001.
9. C. Loring Brace and George Gill, *PBS/NOVA Does Race Exist?* Anthropologists sound off on the issue, December 10, 2002.
10. Erica Frankenberg, Chungmei Lee, and Gary Orfiled, "A Multiracial Society with Segregated Schools: Are We Losing the Dream?" The Civil Rights Project, Harvard University, January 2003.

At Last

1. Lynette Clemetson, "Younger Blacks Tell Democrats to Take Notice," *New York Times,* August 8, 2003, p. A1.
2. See note 1.

Index

Index